THE COINS OF INDIA

THE COINS OF INDIA

C. J. BROWN

GYAN

Published by

Gyan Publishing House
5, Ansari Road
Daryaganj, New Delhi-110002
Phone: 011-47034999, 9811692060
E-mail: books@gyanbooks.com

Distribution Network
gyanbooks.com
India, USA, Canada, UK, Australia

ISBN: 978-93-7169-582-4 (HB)

First Published, 1922

2nd Impression 2025

Printed at: Gyan Press, Delhi.

THE COINS OF INDIA
Author: C. J. BROWN

THE HERITAGE OF INDIA SERIES

THE COINS OF INDIA

BY

C. J. BROWN, M.A.

READER IN ENGLISH LITERATURE, LUCKNOW UNIVERSITY;
MEMBER OF THE NUMISMATIC SOCIETY OF INDIA.

With Twelve Plates

"Time, which antiquates antiquities, and hath an art to make dust of all things, hath yet spared these minor monuments."

—SIR THOMAS BROWNE, *Hydriotaphia*.

ASSOCIATION PRESS
(Y.M.C.A.)
5, RUSSELL STREET, CALCUTTA

LONDON: OXFORD UNIVERSITY PRESS
NEW YORK, TORONTO, MELBOURNE
BOMBAY, CALCUTTA AND MADRAS
1922

CONTENTS

LIST OF PLATES

The Key to each Plate will be found on the page facing it.

INTRODUCTION

This little book has been written as an introduction to the study of the subject with which it deals, and is intended primarily for Indian readers. At the same time the writer trusts it may be of some service to students and collectors, in India and elsewhere, as giving a general conspectus of all the more important series of Indian coins. Two objects have been kept prominently in view: (1) to describe the evolution of the coinage itself, (2) to show its importance as a source of history, or as a commentary upon economic, social and political movements. In attempting this, certain limits have naturally imposed themselves. Coins purely foreign in fabric, as those of the Græco-Bactrian kings, of the Portuguese, and of the various European trading companies, even when struck and current in India, have been rigidly excluded: this exclusion does not, however, extend to money issued by resident foreigners with the permission and in the style of Indian rulers. For a cognate reason the year 1857 has been fixed as the downward limit in this survey. Again, for the sake of simplicity, technical topics, such as weight-standards and metallurgy, have only been touched upon where discussion appeared unavoidable.

The chief desire of the writer has been to arouse in Indians an interest in their country's coinage, in the study of which so many fields of research lie as yet almost untouched. Although India has no coins to show comparable to the supreme artistic conceptions of the Sicilian Greeks, the study of her coinage, in addition to its exceptional importance as a source of history, is attended by peculiar advantages, not the least of which is the fact that materials for study lie, as it were, almost at one's door. In nearly every Indian bazar, even the smallest, in the shops of the *Sarrafs* or money-changers, gold, silver and copper coins are to be had, sometimes in plenty, and can be bought cheaply, often at little more than the metal value. There is even the chance of obtaining for a few coppers, and—a far more important consideration—saving from the melting pot, a coin which may add a new fact, or a name, or a date to history.

A detailed description will be found opposite each of the plates, giving transliterations and translations of the coin legends; and these, with the list of selected authorities at the end of the book, should provide the key to a fuller knowledge of the subject. To almost all the works mentioned in the latter the writer is indebted, although it has been impossible to acknowledge all obligations in detail. Mention must also be made of Dr. George Macdonald's fascinating little study, *The Evolution of Coinage* (The Cambridge Manuals of Science and Literature), as well as of the late Dr. Vincent Smith's *Oxford History of India*, which has in general been accepted as the authority for the historical facts and dates, somewhat plentifully incorporated throughout the book.

In conclusion, I am under special obligation to Mr. John Allan, of the Department of Coins and Medals, British Museum, for continual assistance, for kindly reading through my manuscript and offering numerous useful suggestions, and particularly for his help in getting casts prepared for the plates, all of which have been taken from coins in the British Museum; to Mr. H. Nelson Wright, I.C.S., who also kindly read through the manuscript, gave me invaluable assistance in the transliteration of the coin legends, and freely placed at my disposal his exact and extensive knowledge of the Muhammadan coins of India. To Mr. J. H. Waller, Secretary of the Association Press, I am also considerably indebted for the infinite trouble he has taken in supervising the preparation of the blocks for both figures and plates which illustrate this little volume.

Ranikhet, C. J. BROWN.
May, 1921.

NOTE.—*The Cambridge History of India*, Volume I, Ancient India, appeared while this book was in the press. Fortunately, it has been possible to incorporate the conclusions arrived at in that work, which have been accepted for the period which it covers. The view of the Indo-Greek and later coinages taken by Professor Rapson in Chapters XXII and XXIII has also been generally accepted as a working hypothesis.

ABBREVIATIONS

Anno Domini	A.D.
Copper	Æ.
Hijrī Year	A.H.
Silver	AR.
Gold	AV.
Billon	Bil.
British Museum Catalogue	*B.M.C.*
Grains	Grs.
Indian Antiquary	*I.A.*
Indian Museum Catalogue	*I.M.C.*
Journal of the Asiatic Society of Bengal	*J.A.S.B.*
Journal of Bombay Branch of the Royal Asiatic Society	*J.B.B.R.A.S.*
Journal of the Royal Asiatic Society	*J.R.A.S.*
Numismatic Chronicle	*Num. Chron.*
Numismatic Supplement to the J.A.S.B.	*Num. Supp.*
Obverse	Obv.
Catalogue of Coins in the Panjab Museum, Lahore	*P.M.C.*
Regnal Year	R.
Reverse	Rev.
Samvat Year	S.
Weight	Wt.

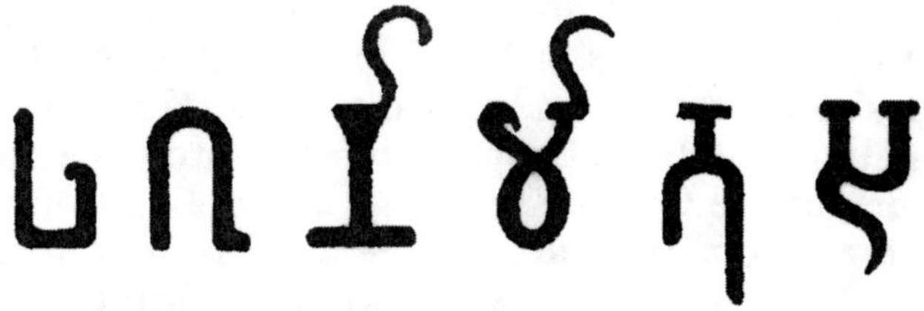

Fig. 1. *Phagunimitrasa* in Early Brāhmī Script. Cf. Pl. I, 4.

I

THE EARLIEST COINAGE OF INDIA

AMONG primitive peoples trade was carried on by barter, that is, exchange in kind. Gradually, with the spread of civilising influences the inconvenience of promiscuous exchange made itself felt, and certain media were agreed upon and accepted by the community at large. Wealth in those early times being computed in cattle, it was only natural that the ox or cow should be employed for this purpose. In Europe, then, and also in India, the cow stood as the higher unit of barter. At the lower end of the scale, for smaller purchases, stood another unit which took various forms among different peoples—shells, beads, knives, and where those metals had been discovered, bars of copper or iron. In India the cowrie-shell, brought from the Maldive Islands, was so employed, and is still to be seen in many bazars in the shops of the smaller money-changers. The discovery of the precious metals carried the evolution of coinage a stage further: for the barter unit was substituted its value in metal, usually gold. The Greek *stater* and the Persian *daric* certainly, and possibly the Indian *suvarna*, so frequently mentioned by Sanskrit authors, was the value of a full-grown cow in gold, calculated by weight. However this may be, in ancient India gold dust, washed out of the Indus and other rivers, served the purposes of the higher currency, and from 518 B.C. to about 350 B.C., when an Indian province or satrapy was included in the Achæmenid Empire of Persia, 360 talents in gold dust was, Herodotus tells us,[1] paid annually as tribute from the province into the treasury of the Great King.

Silver from natural sources was at that time less plentiful in India, but was attracted thither in large quantities in exchange for gold, which was cheaper there than elsewhere in the ancient world. The transition from metal weighed out to the required amount to pieces of metal of recognized weight and fineness regularized by the stamp of authority is not difficult of explanation. The great convenience of the latter would recommend them at once to the merchant, and to the ruler as the receiver of tribute and taxes. Both in Asia and Europe this transition can be illustrated from extant specimens; but, whereas in Europe and Western Asia, from the inscriptions which appeared early on the coins themselves and from outside evidence, we know the origin of the earliest coins and the names of the cities or districts which issued them, the origin of India's earliest coinage, like so much of her early history, is still shrouded in mystery.

This much can be said, that in its earliest stages the coinage of India developed much on the same lines as it did on the shores of the Aegean. Certain small ingots of silver, whose only mark is three circular dots, represent probably the earliest form: next in order are some heavy bent bars of silver with devices stamped out with a punch on one side.[2] These two classes of coins are computed to have been in circulation as coins at least as early as 600 B.C., but they have not been found in any quantity. The time as well as the territory in which they circulated was probably therefore restricted. On the other hand, from almost every ancient site in India, from the Sundarbans in Bengal to

[1] Herod III, 94. Quoted in Cunningham, *Coins of Ancient India*, p. 12.

[2] Cf. *I.M.C.*, p. 136, Nos. 1, 2, 3 (ingots), Nos. 4, 5, 6 (bars).

Kābul, and as far south as Coimbatore, have been recovered thousands of what are known to numismatists as "Punch-marked coins" and to Sanskrit authors as *Purāṇas* ("ancient") or *Dharaṇas*. These are rectangular (Pl. I, 2) and circular (Pl. I, 1) flat pieces of thin silver (much alloyed), or more rarely copper, cut from a hammered sheet of metal and clipped to the proper weight. One side (the obverse) is occupied by a large number of symbols impressed on the metal by means of separate punches. In the oldest coins the other, the reverse side, is left blank, but on the majority there appears usually one, sometimes two or three, minute punch marks; a few coins have both obverse and reverse covered with devices. These devices appear in wonderful variety—more than three hundred have been enumerated; they comprise human figures, arms, trees, birds, animals, symbols of Buddhist worship, solar and planetary signs. Much further detailed study of these coins will be needed before anything can be definitely stated about the circumstances under which they were minted. It seems probable that in India, as in Lydia, coins were first actually struck by goldsmiths or silversmiths, or perhaps by communal gilds (*seṇī*). Coins with devices on one side only are certainly the oldest type, as the rectangular shape, being the natural shape of the coin when cut from the metal sheet, may be assumed to be older than the circular; on the other hand, both shapes, and also coins with devices on one as well as on both sides, are found in circulation apparently at the same time. It has also been recently shown[1] that groups of three, four, and sometimes five, devices on the obverse are constant to large numbers of coins circulating within the same district. It may perhaps therefore be conjectured that the "punch-marked" piece was a natural development of the paper *hundī*, or note of hand; that the coins had originally been struck by private merchants and gilds and had subsequently

[1] By Dr. Spooner, Dr. Bhandarkar, and E. H. Walsh. Cf. *Journal of the Bihar and Orissa Research Society*, 1919, pp. 16-72, 463-94.

passed under royal control; that they at first bore the seal of the merchant or gild, or combination of gilds, along with the seals of other gilds or communities who accepted them;[1] and that, when they passed under regal control, the royal seal and seals of officials were first added to, and afterwards substituted for, the private or communal marks. Be that as it may, we see here in the very earliest coinage the commencement of that fascination which the square coin seems to have exercised upon Indian moneyers of all periods; for it continually reappears, in the coins of the Muhammadan kingdoms of Mālwā and Kashmīr for example, in some beautiful gold and silver issues of the Mughals, Akbar and Jahāngīr, and even in the nineteenth century in copper pieces struck by the Bahāwalpūr State in the Panjāb. Most writers agree, as indeed their shape, form, and weight suggest, that the "punch-marked" coins are indigenous in origin, and owe nothing to any foreign influence. In what part of India they originated we do not know: present evidence and the little knowledge we possess of the state of India in those times indicate some territory in the north. As to the period during which they were in active circulation we are not left so completely at the mercy of conjecture. Finds and excavations tell us something: contemporary writers, Indian and foreign, drop us hints. Sir John Marshall records, during the recent excavations round Taxila, the find of 160 "punch-marked" coins of debased silver, with a coin in fine condition of Diodotos of Bactria (circ. 245 B.C.).[2] Then there is the interesting statement of the usually trustworthy Latin writer, Quintus Curtius, that Omphis (Āmbhi) presented "Signati argenti LXXX talenta"—"80 talents of stamped silver"—to Alexander at Taxila. These and similar pieces of evidence show us that "punch-marked" coins were well established in Northern India during

[1] Even in Mughal times bankers were in the habit of placing their mark on the rim or even on the face of coins which passed through their hands.

[2] *Guide to Taxila*, p. 117.

the fourth and third centuries B.C., when the great Maurya Empire was at the height of its power. The large quantities continually being unearthed suggest a long period of circulation, so that in their earliest forms "punch-marked" coins may go back to the sixth century, and may have remained current in some districts of the north as late as the second century B.C. At some period, perhaps during the campaigns of the great Chandragupta and the settlement of the Empire under his grandson Aśoka, these coins became the established currency of the whole Indian peninsula, and in the southern districts, at least, they must have remained in circulation for three, perhaps four, centuries longer than in the north, for in Coimbatore district "punch-marked" coins have been found along with a *denarius* of the Roman Emperor Augustus; and some of the earliest individualistic coinages of the south, which apparently emerge at a much later period, the so-called "padmaṭaṅkas," for instance, seem to be the immediate successors of these "punch-marked" coins.

Now the distinction between north and south which has just been drawn in tracing the history of this primitive coinage is very important; for this same distinction enables us to divide the remaining ancient and mediæval Indian coins down to the fourteenth century into two classes, northern and southern. The reason for this is that Northern India, during that period, was subjected to a series of foreign invasions; the indigenous coinages of the north were therefore continually being modified by foreign influences, which, with a few exceptions to be noted, left the coinages of the south untouched, to develop by slow stages on strictly Indian lines. The coins of the south will be described in a separate chapter.

To return to Northern India: at the time of Alexander's invasion the whole of North-Western India and the Panjāb was split up into a number of small states, some, like the important state of Taxila, ruled by a king, others governed by "aristocratic oligarchies." Almost all the coins about to be dealt with are either of copper or brass, and the earliest of them were struck, doubtless, by the ruling authorities in these states. Even after their subjection to the great Maurya Emperors some of these states may have retained their coining rights, for it is a salient fact in the history of coins that coinage in the base metals in India and elsewhere has not, until quite recent times, been recognized, like coinage in gold and silver, as the exclusive privilege of the ruler. A striking example is afforded in the copper token money issued by private tradesmen in England during the eighteenth and early nineteenth centuries. On the break up of the Maurya Empire, at the close of the third century, a number of small independent kingdoms sprang into existence, and these proceeded to issue coins, some bearing evident traces of foreign influence, but on the whole following Indian models closely enough to be included here.

No attempt can be made to deal with this class of coins exhaustively: a few typical examples only can be selected for description and illustration. The reader who wishes to pursue the subject further is referred for guidance to the Bibliography at the end of this book; and, since at present little attempt has been made to classify or examine these coins in any detail, fewer fields of research are likely to yield a richer reward to the patient student.

The earliest of these copper coins, some of which may be as early as the fifth century B.C., were cast. The casting of coins by pouring molten metal into a cavity formed by joining two moulds together must have been a very ancient practice in India. Sometimes the moulds of several coins were joined together for the casting process, and the joins thus left are not infrequently found still adhering to the coins (Pl. I, 3).[1] These coins are for the most part anonymous.

[1] This process was in operation in Morocco until the middle of the nineteenth century. Nearchus, the companion of Alexander, says that the Indians used only cast bronze but not hammered. Strabo XV, C. 716.

Even after striking from dies had superseded this clumsy method in the North-West, we find cast coins being issued at the close of the third century by the kingdoms of Kauśāmbī, Ayodhyā and Mathurā, some of which bear the names of local kings in the Brāhmī[1] script.

The earliest die-struck coins, with a device on one side of the coin only, have been assigned to the end of the fourth century B.C. Some of these, with a lion device, were certainly struck at Taxila, where they are chiefly found. Others present various Buddhist symbols, such as the *bodhi-tree*, *svastika*, or the plan of a monastery, and may therefore belong to the time of Aśoka, when Buddhism first reached the North-West, or Gandhāra, as the territory was then called. The method of striking these early coins was peculiar, in that the die was impressed on the metal when hot, so that a deep square incuse, which contains the device, appears on the coin. A similar incuse appears on the later double-die coins of Pañchāla (Pl. I, 4), Kauśāmbī, and on some of Mathurā. This method of striking may have been introduced from Persia, and was perhaps a derivative from the art of seal-engraving.

In the final stage of die-striking, devices were impressed on both sides of the coin, and the best of these "double-die" coins show not only greater symmetry of shape, either round or square, but an advance in the art of die-cutting. Some of the earliest of this type have been classed as gild tokens. The finest were struck in Gandhāra: among these one of the commonest, bearing a lion on the obverse, and an elephant on the reverse (Pl. I, 5), is of special importance, since an approximate date can be assigned to it, for it was imitated by the Greek princes, Pantaleon (Pl. II, 2)

[1] Brāhmī (Fig. 1), Phœnician in origin, was the native script of Northern India, and was written from left to right. Kharoshṭhī (Fig. 2) was a derivation from the Aramaic script, and was written from right to left; it is believed to have been introduced during the Persian domination of Western India, and continued in use on the North-West frontier until about the fourth century A.D.

and Agathokles, who reigned on the North-West frontier about the middle of the second century B.C. In the execution and design of some die-struck coins from the North-West there are undoubted traces of foreign influences: but such devices as the humped bull, the elephant and the religious symbols are purely Indian. There is, on the other hand, little foreign influence traceable in the die-struck coins, all closely connected in point of style, which issued during the first and second centuries B.C. from Pañchāla, Ayodhyā, Kauśāmbī and Mathurā. A number of these bear Brāhmī inscriptions, and the names of ten kings, which some would identify with the old Śuṅga dynasty, have been recovered from the copper and brass coins of Pañchāla, found in abundance at Rāmnagar in Rohilkhand, the site of the ancient city Ahichhatra. Similarly twelve names of kings appear on the Mathurā coins, but we have little knowledge of these kingdoms beyond what the coins supply. Certain devices are peculiar to each series: thus most of the Ayodhyā coins have a humped bull on the obverse, the coins of Kauśāmbī a tree within a railing.

In the coins of Eraṇ[1] we have an illustration, as Rapson says, "of the development of the punch-marked system into the die system." These coins are rectangular copper pieces (Pl. I, 6), and the device on each consists of a collection of symbols like those which appear on the "punch-marked" coins, but struck from a single die. They are specially interesting in that they represent the highest point of perfection reached by purely Indian money. Some of these, in common with a class of round coins found at Ujjain (Avanti), display a special symbol, the "cross and balls," known from its almost universal occurrence on the coins of ancient Mālwā as the Mālwā or Ujjain symbol.

Though its territory lay partially in Southern India, it will be convenient to include here the coinage of the

[1] Eraṇ, or Erakina, the capital of the ancient East Mālwā kingdom, in the Saugor district, Central Provinces.

great Andhra dynasty, since several of its issues are closely connected with the currency of the north. The Andhras probably became independent about the year 230 B.C., and their rule lasted for four and a half centuries. Their coins of various types have been found in Mālwā, on the banks of the Krishna and Godavari rivers, the original home of the race, as far south as Madras, in north Konkan, and elsewhere in the Deccan and the Central Provinces. The earliest to which a date can be assigned are those bearing the name of a king Śrī Sāta, about 150 B.C. Most Andhra coins are either of billon[1] or lead, with Brāhmī legends on both obverse and reverse, and characteristic devices are the elephant, *chaitya* (Buddhist chapel), and bow (Pl. I, 7). Sometimes the "Ujjain symbol" appears on the reverse. One issue, in lead, of Vasishṭhīputra Śrī Pulumāvi (about A.D. 130) is interesting, in that it has on the obverse a ship with two masts, and was evidently intended for circulation on the Coromandel coast. Coins have been assigned to seven Andhra kings, the latest of which, Śrī Yajña Sātakarṇī (about A.D. 184), struck not only the usual lead and billon coins, but restruck and imitated the silver hemidrachms of the satrap Nahapāna (Pl. III, 1). The Andhra lead coinage was copied by one or two feudatory chiefs in Mysore and North Kanara.

[1] Billon, or potin, is a mixture of silver and copper in varying proportions.

Fig. 2. Greek Script on Coin of Hippostratos. Cf. Pl. II, 5.

II

COINS OF THE INDO-GREEKS, THE ŚAKAS AND PAHLAVAS

We have seen in the last chapter how foreign influences gradually began to make themselves felt in the fabric and design of the purely native coins of the North-West. These influences gradually widened until the whole of Northern, Western and parts of Central India were affected. Through eight centuries these foreign types were reproduced on the coins of those territories; and we can observe the gradual debasement of the original models as they become less and less intelligible to successive strikers, until they disappear in the general cataclasm that succeeded the terrible inroads of the Huns in the sixth century. In the secluded kingdom of Kashmīr one type did indeed survive as late as the fifteenth century, a mere shadow of a shade, from which all form and feature had vanished. The coins included in this chapter and the next are those of the invaders who brought about this important change.

But a further and a greater importance attaches to them. Since the important discovery, in 1824, by Colonel Tod, that Greek coins had once been struck in India, the names of thirty-three Greek and twenty-six[1] Indo-Scythian or Śaka and Indo-Parthian or Pahlava princes, ruling territories round the Indian frontier, have gradually been recovered from coin legends, and not more than half-a-dozen of these are known from other sources. Even the names of the later Kushāṇa kings were first deciphered from their coins. Thus coins alone have been responsible for the recovery of a whole period of Indian history.

Probably no class of Indian coins has attracted more attention or been subjected to more patient examination than these, which mark the first intermingling of Eastern and Western culture in India; yet, as the relationship of the different kings and dynasties who minted them, their dates, and the territories over which they ruled are still largely matters of conjecture, it will be well to sketch in outline the probable course which events took in Northern India and the adjacent countries from the time of Alexander to the first century of our era.

In October, 326 B.C., Alexander began his retreat from the Panjāb. To commemorate his victories he struck a medal;[2] about the same time an Indian prince, Sophytes (Saubhūti), struck a silver coin (Pl. II, 1) in the Greek style; with these two exceptions scarcely a mark or lasting trace of his invasion remained. Eleven years after Alexander's death his general, Seleucos, founded the Seleucid kingdom of Syria. Between the years 250-248 B.C. two of the chief Syrian provinces revolted and became independent kingdoms, Bactria under Diodotos and Parthia under Arsakes, both events fraught with important consequences for India and her coinage. The fourth Bactrian king, Demetrios (c. 190-150 B.C.), son of Euthydemos, as the Mauryan Empire fell into decay, was able to extend his kingdom as far as the Panjāb, and assumed the title of "King of the Indians." But about the same time he was confronted with a rival, Eukratides (c. 175-155 B.C.), who deprived him of his Bactrian dominions, and even of a

[1] Three fresh names have been added as recently as 1913.

[2] The sole example known is in the British Museum: it is figured in Vincent Smith's *Oxford History of India*, 1920, p. 63.

portion of Gandhāra (the present districts of Peshāwar and Rawalpindi). Henceforward there were two rival Greek dynasties, the house of Eukratides, including the princes Heliokles, Antialkidas and Hermaios, ruling in Kābul, Kandahār and Gandhāra, and the house of Euthydemos, of whom the principal rulers were Apollodotos, Menander, Strato I, Zoilos and Hippostratos, in East Gandhāra and the Panjāb. Pantaleon, Agathokles and Antimachos, of the latter family, appear to have been petty princes ruling north of Kābul (c. 155-140 B.C.), and there must have been similar small principalities elsewhere, whose rulers were contemporary. About the year 135 B.C. Heliokles, the last king of Bactria, was driven out of that country by a Scythian tribe, the Śakas, and fixed the headquarters of his rule at Kābul, and here his descendants continued to reign till some time after 40 B.C., when the last of them, Hermaios, was driven out by the Pahlavas. Meanwhile, in about the year 126 B.C., the Śakas, pressed in their turn by another nomadic tribe from Central Asia, the Yueh-chi, were driven out of Bactria, and invaded India by way of Ariāna (Herāt) and Drangiāna (Seistān), fixing their headquarters in Sind (Śakadvīpa). Moving thence up the Indus valley, about the year 75 B.C., their chief, Maues, captured Pushkalāvatī (Peshāwar), and thus drove a wedge in between the dominions of the two Greek houses. His successor, Azes I, the possible founder of the Vikrama era in 58 B.C., finally crushed the house of Euthydemos, in the person of Hippostratos, in the Eastern Panjāb, some time after 40 B.C. Closely related to the Śakas were the Pahlavas. The earlier Pahlava princes, Vonones, Spalahores, and Spalirises ruled in Drangiāna and Arachosia (Kandahār), whence, as already related, they overran Kābul. Later on, in the first century A.D., probably through a family alliance, they succeeded the Śakas in northern India and we find the great king Gondopharnes (A.D. 19-45) ruling in Taxila. Associated with the Śaka and Pahlava kings were a number of military governors, such as Aspavarma and Sasas, whose names appear on coins with those of their suzerains. Other rulers like Miaos are more difficult to place.

I. COINS OF THE INDO-GREEKS

The splendid series of portrait coins of the Greek kings of Bactria does not come within the scope of this work: their gold and silver pieces, struck on the Attic standard,[1] were never current in India proper, where they are rarely found, and they really belong to the history of Greek coinage. Nevertheless they are of the utmost importance for our subject, for in following these models the Indo-Greek kings introduced Greek types, and among them the portrait head, into the Indian coinage, and their example was followed for eight centuries. This word "type" needs some definition. Originally it meant the particular mark of authority on a coin as distinct from other marks, but it has come to imply a distinguishing device more or less artistic in character. Such devices appear on all Greek and Roman coins. In this sense the coins of the Muhammadans cannot properly be said to display "types," for both obverse and reverse are usually occupied entirely by the inscription.

Demetrios was the first Bactrian king to strike square copper coins of the Indian type, with a legend in Greek on the obverse, and in Kharoshṭhī on the reverse. His rival, Eukratides, struck these bilingual square copper pieces in greater abundance, as well as a very rare silver coin with inscriptions in both languages. The

[1] On the Attic standard, adopted by Alexander, the Seleucid and Bactrian kings, the drachm weighed 67·5 grains; on the Persian standard, adopted by the Indo-Greeks (and hence in some works called the Indian standard), it weighed 88 grains, but their coins rarely reach the full weight. Mr. Whitehead, in a recent monograph, "The Pre-Muhammadan Coinage of North-Western India" (*Numismatic Notes and Monographs*, No. 13, The American Numismatic Society, New York, 1922), calls the two silver denominations of the Indo-Greeks drachms and tetradrachms, thus supposing a separate Indian standard. I have retained the hitherto accepted nomenclature, hemidrachms and didrachms for convenience of reference to standard works.

Gandhāra copper coinage of Agathokles and Pantaleon (Pl. II, 2) has already been alluded to. After the removal of the seat of government to territory south of the Hindu Kush, we find the coinage undergoing a radical change. The rare gold staters and the splendid tetradrachms of Bactria disappear. The silver coins of the Indo-Greeks, as these later princes may conveniently be called, are the didrachm (Pl. II, 5) and the hemidrachm. With the exception of certain square hemidrachms of Apollodotos and Philoxenos (Pl. II, 7), they are all round, are struck to the Persian (or Indian) standard, and all have inscriptions in both Greek and Kharoshṭhī characters. Copper coins, square for the most part, are very numerous (Pl. II, 6). The devices are almost entirely Greek, and must have been engraved by Greeks, or Indians trained in the Greek traditions, yet "the engravers . . . were no slavish copyists of Western models, but were giving free and spontaneous expression to their own ideas."[1] On the reverse is ordinarily to be found some god or goddess—Herakles, Zeus, Pallas, or some symbol of their worship; the "two piloi" (caps) of the Dioskouroi are of frequent occurrence. A notable square copper coin of Eukratides has the figure of a seated Zeus, accompanied by the legend in Kharoshṭhī, "*The city deity of Kāpiśī*," suggesting that others of these deities may stand as the patrons of cities.[2] Other reverse devices are the tripod, a king on horseback, and various animals, including the specially Indian elephant and humped bull. The portraits on the obverse, especially on the fine didrachms, are realistic and boldly drawn, and show us clearly what manner of men these early European rulers in India were. On most of these coins and those of the Śaka rulers are found a great variety of monograms (Fig. 3) formed of Greek letters, but the significance of these has never been satisfactorily explained. From a study of monograms and types,

[1] Marshall, *Guide to Taxila*, p. 27.

[2] For other city types see *Camb. History of India*, Vol. I, p. 557 *sq.*

and particularly from observing the gradual debasement in style which takes place, experts have been able to arrange these kings in chronological order. Such tests are sometimes, however, delusive; the king, Zoilos, for example, minted two types of hemidrachm, one in comparatively fine style, the other very debased.

The extreme rarity of the money of a few kings, like Apollophanes, Polyxenos and Theophilos, leads us to suppose that they were pretenders. The most important kings, judging from the large number of their coin-types, were Antialkidas, king of Taxila, circ. 155-130 B.C., Apollodotos, Menander and Strato I. Antialkidas appears on one of his numerous silver types wearing the striking flat cap, called "kausia" (Pl. II, 8). Apollodotos' coinage is remarkable for the large variety of its copper types. Particularly noticeable are the large round pieces which he introduced (Pl. II, 3). Menander's coins (Pl. II, 4) are found all over Northern India in great quantities, and his didrachms, with three distinct styles of portrait, are the finest of the series. The heads of two queens, Agathokleia and Kalliope, are found conjoined, the former with that of her son, Strato I, the latter with that of her husband, Hermaios (Pl. II, 9), on a few rare coins. The debasement which set in in Strato's reign (Pl. II, 10) in the Eastern Kingdom, and is evidenced not only in the poorness of design but even in the striking of coins in lead, reached even a lower point in the coinage of Hermaios. On one type of copper, with the head of Hermaios on the obverse, the name of Kujūla Kadphises, the Kushāṇa, appears on the reverse (Pl. IV, 1).[1]

II. COINS OF THE ŚAKAS AND PAHLAVAS

After the conquest of Bactria by the Śakas in 135 B.C. there must have been considerable intercourse,

[1] It is suggested (*Camb. History of India*, p. 561) that the coins of Hermaios extended over a long period, and that it was these degenerate posthumous coins which Kujūla Kadphises copied.

sometimes of a friendly, sometimes of a hostile character, between them and the Parthians, who occupied the neighbouring territory. This may account for the Parthian influence which appears in certain features on the coins of the Sakas, particularly in the title *Basileōs Basileōn*, "King of Kings," which all these kings, following the example of the Arsacid dynasty, inscribed on the obverse of their coins.

Maues, whose coins are found only in the Panjāb, was the first king of what may be called the Azes group of princes. His silver is not plentiful; the finest type is that with a "biga" (two-horsed chariot) on the obverse, and to this type belongs a square hemidrachm, the only square Śaka silver coin known. His commonest copper coins, with an elephant's head on the obverse and a "caduceus" (staff of the god Hermes) on the reverse (Pl. III, 4), are imitated from a round copper coin of Demetrios. On another copper square coin of Maues the king is represented on horseback. This striking device is characteristic both of the Saka and Pahlava coinage (Pl. III, 7); it first appears in a slightly different form on coins of the Indo-Greek Hippostratos (Pl. II, 5); the Gupta kings adopted it for their "horseman" type, and it reappears in Mediæval India on the coins of numerous Hindu kingdoms, and was even employed by Muhammadan invaders until the fourteenth century.

Silver coins of Azes I and Azilises, especially of the former, are abundant. As on Maues' coinage, Greek gods and goddesses, Zeus, Herakles, Pallas and Poseidon, appear on both silver and copper of these two kings, but now for the first time an Indian goddess, Lakshmī, is introduced. A favourite device on the silver of Azilises is the Dioskouroi (Pl. III, 9).[1] His copper coins are all square, whereas Azes' commonest type is a large round coin with a bull on the observe and a lion on the reverse (Pl. III, 5), unquestionably copied from

[1] They are also represented on horseback as on Eukratides' coins.

the large round coins of Apollodotos; for some of Azes I's coins are restruck on those of Apollodotos and Hippostratos. Another copper coin shows the king Azes sitting cross-legged in the Indian fashion. On the reverse of another copper coin, of the common "king on horseback" type, appears the name of the Indian general, Aspavarma, which is also found on some coins of the Pahlava Gondopharnes: this is a most important piece of evidence, as it shows a connection between the two dynasties. The earlier Pahlava kings, which we may call the Vonones group, were evidently far less powerful than the Śaka rulers; their coins are scarcer, didrachms particularly so, and are found only west of the Indus valley. On no coins has the name of Vonones been found alone, but always associated either with Spalahores, his brother, or his nephew, Spalagadames; the names of the two latter are conjoined on another coin (Pl. III, 10). A fourth prince, Spalirises, strikes coins of his own and also in conjunction with Azes II.[1] All the silver coins of this group are of the usual "king on horseback" type; their copper coins are with one exception square.

Like the Indo-Greeks, the Śakas use Greek for the obverse and Kharoshṭhī for the reverse legend.

The most important of the later Pahlava kings was Gondophares, or Gondopharnes, famous as the King of India mentioned in the traditional stories connected with the Apostle St. Thomas. In the British Museum there is a silver coin of his struck in the pure Parthian style, but the rest of his didrachms—no smaller coins are known—are of billon (Pl. III, 8). Several types of these are known, but all have the usual "king on horseback" obverse. On the reverse of one type the god Śiva appears. His copper coins, all of them round, have a bust of the king in the Parthian style, with either a figure of Nike or Pallas on the reverse. The coins of his successors or contemporaries, Abdagases, Orthagnes and Pakores, closely follow in type those of Gondopharnes.

[1] This coin seems to provide the family link between the Śakas and Pahlavas.

Connected with these later Pahlavas are a few princes who call themselves "Satrap"—among these the most prominent is Zeionises, who minted some rather striking didrachms in pure silver. His not uncommon copper coins imitate the bull and lion type of Azes. Lastly, there are a number of miscellaneous rulers, such as Miaos and Hyrcordes, whose coins present features so heterogeneous that it has been impossible hitherto to assign them ancestry, nationality or even an approximate date. The most important of these is the "nameless king," whose superscription consists of the titles, "*King of Kings, the great Saviour,*" written in Greek only. His coins, all of copper, are well struck, especially the commonest type, which shows a diademed head of the king on the obverse and a horseman on the reverse (Pl. III, 6). On all appears his special symbol, a three-pronged fork (Fig. 3, v).[1]

III. COINS OF THE WESTERN SATRAPS AND OTHER IMITATORS OF THE GREEK MODELS

The coinage of the Indo-Greek kings made a deep impression upon their successors and neighbours, just as the coinage of Bactria had impressed the conquering Śakas, who copied it extensively in that country. The crude coins of Miaos (or Heraos) and of Sapeleizes, two very obscure rulers, are evidently modelled on the issues of Heliokles and Eukratides. Śaka princes, like Maues, as we have seen, while adopting many Greek features, employed a characteristic coinage of their own. On the other hand, we find Rājuvula, one of the Śaka satraps who replaced the Hindu kings of Mathurā in the first century A.D., slavishly copying the billon hemidrachms of Strato II (Pl. I, 8). Nahapāna, a great Śaka conqueror who founded a kingdom in the

[1] It has been suggested with great probability that the title *Sotēr Megas* (Great Saviour) was that of the military governor (*stratēgos*) of Taxila under the Kushāṇas, and that these coins were the anonymous issues of successive *stratēgoi*. Cf. *Camb. History of India*, Vol. I, p. 581.

Western Ghats at about the same period, also reproduced the Greek hemidrachm (Pl. II, 11), as did the Andhra king, Śrī Yajña Gotamīputra (Pl. III, 1). Another Śaka chieftain, Chashṭana, about A.D. 115, founded a kingdom in Mālwā, striking hemidrachms like those of Nahapāna on the Greek model, and resembling most nearly the coins of Apollodotos. The coins of both these princes preserve the remains of Greek characters on the obverse, and on the reverse are inscriptions in both Nāgarī[1] and Kharoshṭhī, but after the death of Chashṭana the Kharoshṭhī inscription disappears. His successors, known as the Western Satraps, extended his dominions by conquests from the Andhras until they embraced all the flourishing ports on the west coast with their valuable sea-borne trade. Their hemidrachms are found in great abundance throughout Western India: on the reverse of all appears the Buddhist *chaitya* copied from the Andhra coinage; the portraits on the obverse are distinctly Scythian in appearance. These coins are of special historical importance; for in the reign of the fifth satrap, Jīvadāman, dates in the so-called Śaka era,[2] recording the year of issue, were added to the inscription (Pl. III, 2); and these are of the greatest service in helping to date events here and elsewhere in India down to the year A.D. 395, when the Guptas conquered the country, and the long and monotonous series of Western Satrap coins came to an end. The Guptas in their turn struck silver of the same type; and these degenerate descendants of the Greek hemidrachm had a further lease of life, when, imported by the Guptas from their western (Pl. VI, 1) to their central dominions (Pl. VI, 2), they were adopted by several minor dynasties, including the Maukharīs, and were even struck by the invading Huns (Pl. VI, 7).

Imitation of both Greek and Śaka models is noticeable in the coins of the Hindu state of Odumbara. (Pl. III, 3), the modern Pathānkot; both these and the

[1] Nāgarī is a later form of Brāhmī script.

[2] The Śaka era started in A.D. 78; this date is now considered to mark the first year of Kanishka's reign.

earlier silver coins of the Kuṇindas, who occupied hilly districts near the river Satlej, have legends in Brāhmī and Kharoshṭhī; both may be assigned to the first century B.C.

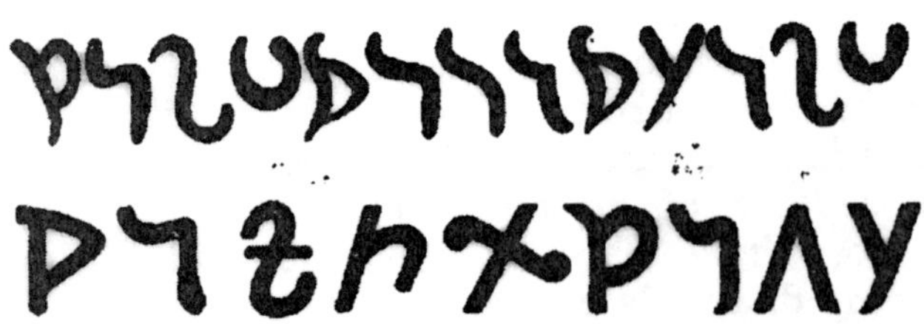

Fig. 3. Kharoshṭhī Script on Coin of Hippostratos. Cf. Pl. II, 5.

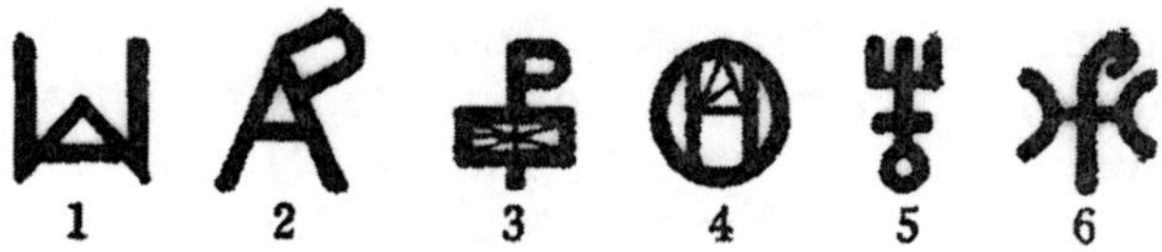

Fig. 3. Monograms on Indo-Greek Coins, etc.

III

COINS OF THE KUSHĀṆA KINGS

THE Yueh-chi, who drove the Śakas out of Bactria about the year 126 B.C., were destined to create "one of the greatest empires of ancient India." At some date after A.D. 25, one of the five tribes of which they were composed, the Kushāṇas, became supreme, and under the leadership of the head of that tribe, Kujūla Kadphises, they passed south of the Hindu Kush, and overwhelmed the Pahlavas, then ruling in the Kābul valley. The deposition of Pacores, successor of Gondopharnes to the Pahlava kingdom of Taxila, must have taken place between the years A.D. 45 and A.D. 64, and was effected by Vima Kadphises, the second Kushāṇa king. Henceforward there is less confusion of dynasties. We know the names and the chronological order of these powerful Kushāṇa princes—Kujūla Kadphises, Vima Kadphises, Kanishka, Huvishka, Vāsudeva; the names of the three last are even recorded in several inscriptions. It seems to be now generally accepted that Kanishka was the founder of the so-called Śaka era, and that consequently his reign started in A.D. 78.[1] The chief remaining difficulty is the attribution of certain copper coins bearing the title *Kujūla*

[1] *Cambs. History of India*, Vol. I, p. 583.

Note.—The monograms in Fig. 3 occur on coins of the following: (1) Eukratides, (2) Apollodotos, (3) Apollodotos, Maues, (4) Azes I, (5) Soter Megas, (6) Gondopharnes and Aspavarma.

Kadaphes (Kharoshṭhī—*Kuyula Kaphasa*); this must remain for the present unsettled.

The commoner type of these Kadaphes coins deserves special attention (Pl. IV, 2); for the head on the obverse is directly copied from the coins of one of the earlier Roman Emperors, probably Augustus, and bears evidence to that Roman influence which is so marked in the gold coinage of the Kushāṇas, and which is partly traceable to the intercourse between the Yueh-chi and the Roman Empire before their invasion of India, an intercourse which resulted in Kushāṇa ambassadors being actually sent to the court of Augustus. But the plentiful issues in gold of Vima Kadphises and his two successors, all struck on the same standard as the Roman *aureus*, are due also to other causes. Exports from India to different provinces of the Roman Empire, carried by sea from the south, and by the overland routes in the north, were paid for in Roman gold; and the *aureus* had, like the English *sovereign* in more recent times, at this period acquired that status as a current coin in India, which it already possessed in those parts of Asia more directly under the influence of the imperial power. It was only natural that these Kushāṇa invaders should seek to win acceptance for their new gold currency by placing it on an equality with the popular Roman gold. There was, moreover, at this time a world shortage of silver: not only do we find the Pahlava kings striking didrachms in debased silver, but the silver *denarius* itself was, during the early empire, being reduced in weight and fineness. This accounts for the disappearance of silver and the important place of gold in the Kushāṇa coinage, and is probably also partly the reason why the Western Satraps struck only small hemidrachms, and these often in inferior silver.

The coins of Kujūla Kadphises are all of copper. Those which he struck in the style of Hermaios have the head of the Greek king on the obverse (Pl. IV, 1), and he used the same type after the name of Hermaios had disappeared from the inscriptions; both these types were current in the Kābul province. Another type, akin to the Śaka coins, has a bull on the obverse and a Bactrian camel on the reverse. In one of his inscriptions, for which like his successor he uses both Greek and Kharoshṭhī, he is styled "*The Great King, King of Kings, the Son of Heaven.*"

The gold of Vima Kadphises (c. A.D. 45-78) was struck in three denominations, the double stater (Pl. IV, 3), the stater or *dināra*,[1] as the Kushāṇas called it (= the Roman *aureus* of 124 grains weight), and the quarter stater. On the obverse of these appears either the king's head or bust, or the king seated cross-legged on a couch, or, as on a rare stater in the British Museum, sitting in a two-horsed chariot. On the copper coins, which are of three sizes, the king is almost invariably standing, with his right hand placing an offering upon a small altar at his side. The portrait of the king is most realistic, though hardly flattering—a corpulent figure with a long heavy face and a large nose, he appears wearing the long Kushāṇa cloak and tall "Gilgit" boots, on his head a conical hat with streamers. Vima Kadphises must have been a zealous convert to the worship of the Hindu god Śiva, for the god or his emblem, the trident battle-axe, is the invariable device on the reverse of all his coins. The title "*Sotēr Megas*" on this king's copper coins indicates a relationship between him and the so-called "nameless king" mentioned in the previous chapter, whose coins bear the same legend.

Kanishka, the real founder of the great Kushāṇa empire, which stretched from Kābul[2] to the banks of the Ganges, may have belonged to another branch of the

[1] *Dināra* is derived from the Roman *denarius*. It affords an interesting example of the vicissitudes which so many coin names have experienced. The first letter of the same word *d* (*enarius*) now signifies copper in English money.

[2] The province of Kābul must be reckoned Indian territory from the time of Chandragupta Maurya till the eleventh century. It was reunited to India by the Mughal Emperor Bābur in the sixteenth century and lost again in the middle of the eighteenth.

Yueh-chi—he was not, at any rate, nearly related to Vima Kadphises, whose coins are distinct in many respects from those of Kanishka and his successors. One marked distinction is the use of Greek legends only by these later kings. The Greek is often very debased, and the reason suggested for its employment is that Khotanese, the native tongue of the Kushāṇas, was first reduced to writing in the Greek character. Kanishka also introduced the Iranian title, *Shāonānoshāo*—"King of Kings"—in place of the Greek form *Basileōs Basileōn*. On the reverse side of the extensive gold (full and quarter staters only) and copper coinage of Kanishka and Huvishka is portrayed a whole pantheon of gods and goddesses; among them are, the Greek gods, Helios, Herakles (Pl. IV, 8), Selene; the Hindu god, Siva (*Oesho* on the coins); the Iranian deities, Athro, "Fire," Oado, the wind god, Ardokhsho and Nāna, and even the great Buddha himself (Pl. IV, 4), who had previously appeared on a copper coin of Kadaphes. The representation of this "mixed multitude" was probably intended to conciliate the religious scruples of the numerous peoples included within the vast territory of the Kushāṇa Empire. A standing figure of the king appears on the obverse of Kanishka's gold staters, on the small quarter staters is a half (Pl. IV, 5) or quarter length portrait. On Huvishka's gold the standing figure never appears; the portrait is either half length or merely the king's head; on one coin the king is seated cross-legged; on another (exceedingly rare) he is riding an elephant (Pl. VI, 7). Vāsudeva closely imitates Kanishka's standing figure type on his gold.

Kanishka's copper coinage is of two types: one has the usual "standing king" obverse (Pl. IV, 6); and on the rarer second type the king is sitting on a throne. Huvishka's copper is more varied; on the reverse, as on Kanishka's copper, there is always one of the numerous deities; on the obverse the king is portrayed (1) riding on an elephant, or (2) reclining on a couch, or (3) seated cross-legged, or (4) seated with arms raised.

Kanishka had been a great patron of Buddhism. Vāsudeva was evidently a convert to Hinduism and an ardent devotee of Śiva. On the reverses of his coins the deity is almost invariably Śiva accompanied by his bull (Pl. IV, 9), but there is a rare copper piece on which the word "Vāsu" in Brāhmī occupies the obverse, and the special symbol of Vāsudeva the reverse. About half a dozen other symbols, which take the place of the monograms of the Indo-Greeks, appear on the coins of the Kushāṇas.

After the death of Vāsudeva, in A.D. 220, the Kushāṇa power declined, though the descendants of Kanishka held the Kābul valley till A.D. 425. The coins of these kings, principally of two classes, are degenerate copies of the gold coins of Kanishka and Vāsudeva. One continues the standing-king type with the Śiva and bull reverse; the second has the standing-king obverse, with the deity Ardokhsho, who was by this time identified with the Indian Lakshmī, represented as sitting on a throne and holding a cornucopia on the reverse (Pl. IV, 10). Certain Brāhmī letters, now unintelligible, seem to have distinguished the coins of successive rulers. It was this latter type, current throughout the Panjāb, that the Gupta kings took as the model for their earliest coinage. In A.D. 425 a tribe of the Little Yueh-chi, under a chief named Kidāra, replaced the great Kushāṇa dynasty at Kābul; but they were driven out fifty years later by an inroad of the Ephthalites, or White Huns, and settled in the Chitrāl district and in Kashmīr. There they struck coins in much alloyed gold and also in copper of this same standing-king and seated-goddess type, and there it survived in a hardly recognizable form in the later coins, until the Muhammadans put an end to the Hindu kingdom in the fourteenth century. Certain kingdoms in the Panjāb also copied the large copper coins of the Kushāṇas: the most striking of these minor coinages is that of the Yaudheyas, whose territory included the modern state of Bahāwalpūr. One type of their coins shows a female standing figure on the obverse, and a soldier with a Brāhmī inscription on the reverse (Pl. IV, 11). The earliest coins of Nepāl current from the fifth to the seventh century also show traces of Kushāṇa influence. These large copper pieces give the names of at least four kings, Mānāṅka, Gunāṅka,[1] Aṅśuvarman and Jishṇugupta. Various devices are used, among them the goddess seated cross-legged. The coins of Aṅśuvarman, of the seventh century, have a cow standing to the left on the obverse and a winged horse with the king's name on the reverse (Pl. V, 1).

The reigns of Kanishka and Huvishka coincide with the most flourishing period of the great Gandhāra school of sculpture, which had arisen during the rule of the Śaka princes. Hellenistic influence is very strongly marked in that art, and it may be interesting to consider here briefly what contribution the coins make to the vexed question of the respective parts played by Greek and Indian ideals in moulding its character. A careful inspection of the successive coinages of the Indo-Greeks, the Śakas and the Kushāṇas will show that the strongest influences of pure Greek art had passed away before the reign of Kanishka. With the establishment of Greek rule south of the Hindu Kush, traces of the Indian craftsman's hand begin to appear. As time goes on these become more apparent, until, in the Kushāṇa period, the whole fabric of the coins, if not entirely Indian, is far more Oriental than Greek. That purely Indian influences were strongly at work is very evident in the cult of Śiva as expressed on the coins of Vima Kadphises and Vāsudeva for instance; in the Buddha coins of Kadaphes and Kanishka, and in the typical Indian cross-legged attitude in which Kadphises II and Huvishka are depicted; and, after all is said, the art was produced in India and must have been largely if not entirely the work of Indian craftsmen. Originality in art does not so much consist in evolving something

[1] It has been suggested with great probability that these are really compound words signifying "the mark or device of Māna, of Guna."

which has never existed before, but rather in the ability to absorb fresh ideas and transmute them into a new form. And thus it was in the time of Kanishka: Indian mysticism allowed itself to be clad in Greek beauty of form. Eastern feeling ran, as it were, into Western moulds to create this wonderful aftermath of Hellenic art, which left an indelible mark upon every country of the Orient where the cult of the Buddha penetrated.

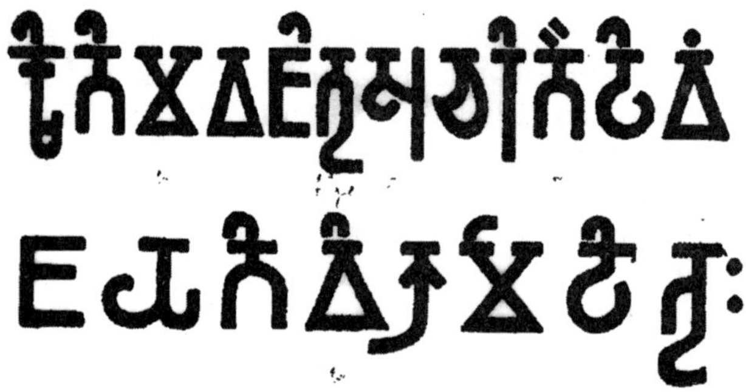

Fig. 4. Gupta Script on coin of Chandragupta II. Cf. Pl. V, 7 (obverse).

IV

THE COINAGE OF THE GUPTAS

THE Gupta period, computing it roughly as lasting from A.D. 320 to 480, synchronises with a great revival of Hinduism, and along with it of literature, the arts and sciences. The Gupta monarchs, as is evident from their coins, although orthodox devotees of Vishṇu, were liberal patrons. Kālidāsa and other writers raised literary Sanskrit to a point of perfection never equalled before or since; the cave frescoes of Ajanta bear witness to the genius of the Gupta painters; the architecture and sculpture of the period show an equally high level of attainment; all the greatest Hindu mathematicians and astronomers flourished in the fifth and sixth centuries. It is, in fact, evident that when the Hindu of to-day harks back to the Golden Age of Hinduism, the picture he draws in his mind is coloured by traditions, which have come to him from books or hearsay, of the age of the Guptas, rather than by the fainter glimmerings of more heroic times from the Vedas or the great Epics. So, too, the splendid gold coinage of the Guptas, with its many types and infinite varieties and its inscriptions in classical Sanskrit, now appearing on Indian coins for the first time, are the finest examples of purely Indian art of this kind we possess.

The origin of the Gupta family is obscure. This much seems certain, that the family was not of high caste, perhaps of the lowest. The territory which the Guptas are first found ruling lay near Pāṭaliputra, the modern Patna; it was much enlarged by one Gupta, on the decline of the Kushāṇa power in its eastern territories; he was succeeded by a son, Ghaṭotkacha, who assumed the title of Mahārāja, which brings us out into the light of history; for with the year of his son Chandragupta I's accession, A.D. 320, the Gupta era starts. It may appear strange that this monarch should have issued no coins of his own, but there seems little reason now to doubt that, to his son and successor, Samudragupta, the real founder of the Gupta Empire, should be assigned those coins (Pl. V, 4) which bear the portraits of Chandragupta and his wife Kumāradevī,[1] a member of the illustrious Lichchavi family reigning at Vaiśālī[2] as early as the seventh century B.C. Samudragupta's conquests, as we learn from his Allahabad pillar inscription, carved out for him an empire which extended north to the base of the Himalayas, east to the Brahmaputra river, south to the banks of the Narbada, and west to the Jumna and the Chambal, with a number of protected states on his frontier between those rivers and the Chināb. On the completion of his conquests he revived an ancient Hindu rite in celebrating the Aśvamedha, or Horse-sacrifice. Now the states under Samudragupta's protection in the Panjāb were the districts of the old Kushāṇa Empire in which the gold coinage current at this time was, as we saw in the last chapter, a degraded form of the Kushāṇa "standing king" and "seated goddess," Ardokhsho-Lakshmī type: it was from these coins (Pl. IV, 10) that the earliest and commonest form of Samudragupta's issues, the Standard type (Pl. V, 2)

[1] Cf. *B.M.C.*, "Coins of the Gupta Dynasties," Introduction, pp. lxiv-lxviii.

[2] Situated in Tirhut, Bengal.

was imitated. The earliest specimens, though much superior in workmanship, follow their model very closely: the "standing king" still wears Kushāṇa dress; a Kushāṇa symbol still appears on the reverse; only, on the obverse, in place of Śiva's trident, appears a Garuḍa-headed standard (*Garuḍadhvaja*), emblem of the cult of Vishṇu. This coinage appears to have been introduced about the middle of the reign: such legends as "*The invincible one, the lord of the earth*" suggest, as indeed is obvious, that only rich plunder made such a varied and plentiful gold currency possible. Samudragupta struck only gold. In such abundance did the Kushāṇa kings mint copper money that it may be said without exaggeration to have remained in circulation in the Panjāb down to the nineteenth century; in the time of the Guptas the bazars must have been full of it. But for gold there is always an insatiable demand in India, and seven other distinct varieties appeared during this reign. Of these the Archer type, the commonest and most characteristic Gupta coin (Pl. V, 6), struck by at least eight succeeding kings, is a natural development of the Standard type, of which also further modifications are to be found in the Battle-axe and Kācha types. On the obverse of the former a second attendant figure is introduced, and a battle-axe instead of a standard is in the king's left hand. In the Kācha coins the change takes place on the reverse, where a standing figure of Lakshmī facing left takes the place of the seated goddess: the reverses of the Tiger-slayer and Aśvamedha coins present variations of this motif. The Tiger-slayer type, of which four specimens only are at present known, is the prototype of the Lion-slayer issues of later kings, and represents the king, dressed for the first time in an Indian waistcoat and turban, trampling on a tiger as he shoots it. There remain the Chandragupta I, Aśvamedha (Pl. V, 5) and Lyrist types, all three obviously in the nature of commemorative medals, and perhaps intended as pious gifts (*dakshiṇa*) to Brahmans. The Lyrist coins (Pl. V, 3), the rarest of the three, merit special attention. Evidently intended as a graceful tribute to the king's accomplishments, he is portrayed in Indian dress, sitting cross-legged on a high-backed rather ornate couch, playing on a *vīṇā*, or Indian lute. On the reverse appears the goddess Lakshmī seated to left on a *mora* (wicker stool). The excellent modelling of the king's figure, the skilful delineation of the features, the careful attention to details, and the general ornateness of design in the best specimens constitute this type as the highest expression of Gupta numismatic art.

Chandragupta II Vikramāditya (= Sun of Power), who succeeded to the throne in A.D. 375, extended still further the boundaries of the empire, and at some time during his long reign, which lasted till A.D. 413, removed the capital from Pāṭaliputra to Ayodhyā. His gold coinage is even more abundant than his father's, two of whose types, the Archer and Lion-slayer (Tiger-slayer), he continued; but on his later Archer coins (Pl. V, 6) the goddess Lakshmī sits upon a lotus instead of a throne; and in the second type, besides the substitution of a lion for a tiger, there is a change on the reverse, Lakshmī being seated on a lion in various attitudes. The figure of the Lion-slayer on the obverse is sometimes turned to the right and sometimes to the left; and a unique coin in the Lucknow Museum shows him attacking the lion with a sword. The very rare Couch design of Chandragupta is a derivative of Samudragupta's Lyrist type. In the new Chattra type coins (Pl. V, 7) we have yet a further variant of the Standard type: on the obverse of these, behind the "standing king," appears a boy or dwarf, holding an umbrella (*chattra*) over his head; the reverse shows the goddess Lakshmī standing on a lotus. An entirely new design is furnished by this king's Horseman coins (Pl. V, 8). A king on horseback was, as we have seen, employed by the Indo-Greeks, and was characteristic of the issues of the Śakas. The Gupta rendering of the motif is new and spirited. The horse is fully caparisoned, facing in some coins to the right, on others to the left, and the king, either fully clad or sometimes only in a waistcoat, carries either a sword or a bow; the reverse resembles that of the Lyrist type.

Kumāragupta I (413-455) struck a few very rare Aśvamedha coins, closely resembling those of Samudragupta, except that they are far inferior in execution, and the sacrificial horse on the obverse is standing to the right instead of to the left.

He also continued to issue the Archer, Horseman and Lion-slayer (Pl. V, 9) types of his predecessors. Kumāragupta's Tiger-slayer coins closely resemble their prototype struck by Samudragupta, except that on the reverse the goddess Lakshmī is depicted feeding a peacock. Four new designs appear on the gold of this reign. The Swordsman coins present still another modification of the Standard type, their distinguishing mark being that the king's left hand rests on his sword-hilt instead of grasping a standard; on the reverse is the usual goddess seated on a lotus. Kumāragupta held the god Kārttikeya, one of whose names was Kumāra, in special veneration. The Peacock type (Pl. V, 10) bears evidence to this, for on the reverse the god himself appears riding on his peacock, Paravāṇi, and on the obverse the king is shown standing and feeding a peacock from a bunch of grapes. The rare Elephant-rider type shows the king on the obverse riding on an elephant trampling on a tiger; and the obverse of the still rarer Pratāpa type, so called from the legend on the reverse, is evidently an adaption from some foreign, probably Roman, model.

Skandagupta, the last of the great Gupta kings, who succeeded his father in A.D. 455, was occupied during the earlier part of his reign in defending his empire against the inroads of the Huns, over whom he appears to have gained a decisive victory. This probably accounts for the comparative scarcity of his gold, of which only two types are known. He continued the favourite device of the Archer with the "seated goddess" reverse, and introduced a new type, on the obverse of which the king appears standing on the left, facing the goddess Lakshmī on the right, with the Garuḍa standard between them. But in this reign the gold coinage underwent an important change of a different character. Hitherto all the Gupta gold pieces had been *dināras* and followed the weight standard adopted by the Kushāṇa kings from the Romans. All Skandagupta's coins are, on an average, heavier than those of his predecessors; and certain of his Archer coins evidently represent a new standard of about 142 grains, based, perhaps, on the ancient Hindu *suvarṇa*; but along with the increase in weight there is a corresponding depreciation in the purity of the gold.

The successors of Skandagupta—Puragupta, Narasiṁhagupta, Kumāragupta II, Chandragupta III and Vishṇugupta, whose relationship and dates are somewhat doubtful, struck gold coins only of the Archer type, showing a gradual deterioration in design and execution. On a few coins of the same type are found portions of names, such as *Ghaṭo* and *Jaya*, even more difficult to identify. A certain Prakāśāditya, perhaps identical with Puragupta, struck coins on which the king appears on horseback slaying a lion, a combination of the Horseman and Lion-slayer types (Pl. V, 11).

The inscriptions on Gupta coins are scarcely inferior to the designs in interest: they vary with each successive type and frequently bear a close relation to them. Thus on Samudragupta's Battle-axe issue the king is described as "*Wielding the axe of Kṛitānta*" (= Yama, the god of Death), while on his Tiger-slayer coins he is given the title *Vyāghraparākramaḥ*, "He who has the prowess of a tiger." Sometimes varieties of the same type are marked by a difference in the inscription: no less than seven different legends are found on Kumāragupta I's Archer coins alone. The obverse legend, which encircles the design, usually takes the form of a verse in *Upagīti* or some other Sanskrit metre, celebrating in highly ornate language the king's glory on the earth and his future bliss in heaven, attained through his merit acquired by sacrifice. On the gold of Samudragupta six such metrical legends appear;

Chandragupta II has only three; while at least twelve are employed by Kumāragupta I. As an example the obverse inscription on one class of Chandragupta II's Chattra coins (Fig. 4) may be taken: "*Vikramāditya, having conquered the earth, wins heaven by good works*"; or the more ornate legend on a variety of Kumāragupta I's Horseman type: "*The unconquered Mahendra, invincible, the moon in the sky of the Gupta line, is victorious.*" When a verse appears on the obverse, the reverse legend is distinct, consisting of a title, sometimes the repetition of one which appears already in the metrical obverse inscription, such as *Apratirathaḥ*, "The invincible one," on the Archer coins of Samudragupta. Sometimes the king's name and titles only appear, and then the legend on both obverse and reverse is often, though not always, continuous, but here again the reverse inscription, which appears to the right of the device, consists of a single title. Thus on Chandragupta II's Archer type appears the following: obverse, *Deva-Śrī-Mahārājādhirāja-Śrī-Chandraguptaḥ*; reverse, *Śrī Vikramaḥ*. Entirely distinct in point of their inscriptions from all other Gupta coins are those struck by Samudragupta in memory of his father and mother, known as the Chandragupta I type; on the obverse appear the two names *Chandragupta* and *Kumāradevī*, and on the reverse his mother's family name, *Lichchavayaḥ*. This relationship was evidently a matter of pride to the striker. Finally, on the obverse of all coins of the Archer and most of the allied types appears vertically, under or near the king's left arm, part of the king's name, as *Samudra*, *Chandra* or *Kumāra*. This vertical method of inscription can be traced back through the later Kushāṇa coins to a Chinese source.[1]

Whether the symbols which occur regularly on all Gupta gold are anything more than ornaments is doubtful.

The silver coinage of the Guptas starts, as has been already noticed, with the overthrow of the Western

[1] Coins have been found in Khotān with a Chinese legend on the obverse and a Kharoshṭhī inscription on the reverse. Cf. *P.M.C.*, Vol. I, p. 167, Nos. 134, 135.

Satraps by Chandragupta II. His issues follow those of the conquered nation very closely, except that on the obverse appears a figure of Vishṇu's sacred bird, Garuḍa, in place of the *chaitya*, and the dates are computed in the Gupta instead of in the Śaka era. Obviously these were intended for circulation in the recently annexed provinces. Kumāragupta, while striking large quantities of the Garuḍa-type coins in the west (Pl. VI, 1), extended the silver coinage to the Central Provinces of his Empire. This latter class of money is entirely distinct in character: the head on the obverse is drawn in a crude but quite original manner, and is probably intended as a portrait of the king; on the reverse the king's devotion to Kārttikeya is once more displayed in the representation of a peacock with outstretched wings. A third class of silver-plated coins, with a rude figure of Garuḍa on the reverse, seems to have been intended for the tributary state of Valabhī.[1] Skandagupta continued the Garuḍa and Peacock types (Pl. VI, 2) of his father, and introduced two new ones. The coins, of very base silver, with Śiva's sacred bull Nandi on the reverse, were probably current in Kathiawar; but commoner than any of the preceding are certain ill-shaped pieces with an altar on the reverse. None of the direct descendants of Skandagupta appears to have struck silver, but a few coins of the Peacock type were issued by Budhagupta, a king of Eastern Mālwā, about A.D. 480. The dates which appear on these coins to the left of the obverse head in the Western, and to the right in the Central, issues are frequently defective or illegible. Inscriptions are confined to the reverse, on the Peacock type always a metrical legend, on all other types the king's name accompanied by high-sounding titles.

The copper coinage, which is practically confined to the reign of Chandragupta II, is far more original in design. Eight out of the nine types known to have

[1] In the Kathiawar peninsula, forming part of what was then known as Surāshṭra.

been struck by him have a figure of Garuḍa on the reverse, usually accompanied by the name of the king, while the obverse is occupied by the bust or head of the king, or by a three-quarter length portrait. In one class this is varied by the reproduction of the gold Chattra type obverse (Pl. V, 13). The tiny coins which constitute the ninth type have the word *Chandra* in the obverse and a flower vase (*kalaśa*) on the reverse. Only four copper pieces are at present known of Kumāragupta.

After the death of Skandagupta, in A.D. 480,[1] the Gupta Empire rapidly broke up. The inferiority and comparative scarcity of his own gold coins, the still more debased issues of his brother Puragupta and subsequent kings, and the disappearance of silver money, bear ample evidence to their curtailed territory.

The impression produced by the magnificent coinage of the Guptas upon the peoples of Northern India was undoubtedly as great as that created by the currency of their Kushāṇa predecessors; but, after the general devastation caused by the inroads of the Huns, few princes could have retained sufficient wealth in their treasuries to imitate it. It is significant then that the most notable imitations were the product of a mint, secured by its remoteness from the ruthless hand of the invader, in Central Bengal. These remarkable and not uncommon coins, with Śiva reclining on his bull Nandi on the obverse, and the goddess Lakshmī seated on a lotus on the reverse (Pl. V, 12), were struck by Śaśāṅka, king of Gauḍa (circ. 600-625), notorious as the assassinator of Harshavardhana's elder brother, and a great "persecutor of Buddhism." In Bengal, too, for many years after the passing of the Gupta Empire, were current flat gold pieces with crude reproductions of Gupta designs, and, with the exception of the word *Śrī* on the obverse, completely illegible inscriptions. Another rather striking coin connected with the Gupta series, with a stand-

[1] Or according to Mr. Panna Lal, "Dates of Skandagupta and His Successors," *Hindustan Review*, January, 1918, in A.D. 467.

ing bull on the obverse, bears the name *Śrī Vīrasena*, but who Vīrasena was is at present unknown. A modification of the seated goddess motif was preserved on the gold coinage of certain mediæval Rājpūt kingdoms.

The western silver coinage of the Guptas may have been imitated by some of the powerful Maitraka rulers of Valabhī, who asserted their independence at the end of the fifth century: coins bearing the name Kṛishṇarāja, at present unidentified, are copied from Skandagupta's bull type. Far more important are the coins struck by Īśānavarman, the Maukhari, and his successors, whose kingdom was in Bihār. These follow the Central Peacock-type, but the head on the obverse, excepting the issue of one king, is turned to the left instead of to the right. These otherwise insignificant coins have a twofold interest: they were copied by the Hun Toramāṇa; and, more important still, the name appearing on the last and most abundant coins of the series is Śilāditya (Pl. VI, 3), who is almost certainly to be identified with the great Harshavardhana of Thāṇeśar and Kanauj, himself a relation of the Maukhari princes. What further strengthens this conjecture is the fact that the dates on the Śilāditya coins are reckoned in a new era, doubtless that which commenced with Harshavardhana's coronation in A.D. 606, whereas the Maukhari kings use the Gupta era. It is striking testimony to the havoc wrought by the Hun invasions that these tiny silver pieces are the only coins[1] known to have been issued by this great king, who built up on the ruins of Northern India an empire scarcely less extensive than that of the Guptas.

The copper money of the Guptas was copied by the Hun princes, Toramāṇa and Mihiragula, but left no legacy behind, unless the small coins which record the names of six Nāga princes of Narwar in Northern Rājputāna may have been derived from it.

[1] Certain thin silver coins of Sassanian type have been doubtfully ascribed to him. Cf. Rapson, *Indian Coins*, p. 34, § 122.

Fig. 5. *Śrī Maj Jajalla-deva*, in old Nāgarī Script.

V

MEDIÆVAL COINAGES OF NORTHERN AND CENTRAL INDIA TILL THE MUHAMMADAN CONQUEST

THE centuries which elapsed between that great turning point in Indian history, the Hun invasions, and the coming of the Muhammadans in the twelfth century, suggest several points of comparison with the so-called Dark Ages of European history. It was an age of transition, pregnant with important developments for the future, but individualistic expression, both in art and literature, remained largely in abeyance. This want of originality is particularly marked in the limited coinage of the numerous petty kingdoms which flourished and declined during the seventh, eighth and ninth centuries. The most important movement of the time was the rise of the Rājpūt clans, which were now emerging as the dominant powers in Hindustān. The Bull and Horseman type in the Rājpūt coinage symbolises this new force. In addition to the issues of the Huns and the Rājpūt dynasties will be described the money of Kashmīr, which, protected by its mountainous frontiers, ordinarily remained shut off from the influence of political events which agitated the kingdoms of the plains.

I. COINS OF THE HUNS AND INDO-SASSANIANS

The military occupation of India by the Huns, or Hūṇas, lasted but thirty years. By A.D. 500 Toramāṇa, leader of the tribe known as the White Huns or Ephthalites, had established himself in Mālwā. On his death, two years later, his successor, Mihiragula, completed the conquest of Northern India, fixing his capital at Śākala (Siālkōt) in the Panjāb, but was driven out by a confederacy of Hindu princes under the leadership of Yasodharman of Mālwā in A.D. 528. He thereupon seized the kingdom of Kashmīr, where he ruled till his death in 542. Probably there were other Hūṇa chiefs who struck coins in India, but the legends on their coins are so fragmentary that their names have not as yet been satisfactorily deciphered. On some of the earliest Hūṇa imitations of Sassanian silver coins, for example, the legend *Shāhī Javūvlaḥ* appears, but whether this is the name of a king or merely a title is uncertain. No Hūṇa coins show any originality of design. The majority are either imitated from or restruck upon Sassanian silver pieces. The heads of both Toramāṇa and Mihiragula (Pl. VI, 4) on the obverse are coarse and brutal to the last degree; on the reverse appear the usual Sassanian fire-altar and attendants; the inscriptions are generally in Nāgarī script. Toramāṇa also copied the silver coinage of the Maukharis (Pl. VI, 7). The copper of both princes show traces of Sassanian and Gupta influence; the reverses especially recall the fabric of Chandragupta II's copper issues. Kushāṇa copper was imitated by Mihiragula, probably during his reign in Kashmīr.

Although the Huns were mainly instrumental in introducing Sassanian types into India, it seems certain that shortly after their invasion a Sassanian dynasty, or a dynasty acknowledging the suzerainty of Persia, was established in Western India; for coins with bilingual inscriptions in Pahlavī and Nāgarī have been found, directly imitated from Sassanian issues. One of these bears the name Shāhī Tigin, and the Nāgarī legend reads, "*King of India and Persia.*" Another class with the name Vāsudeva is directly copied from a type of the coinage of the Sassanian Khusrū Parvīz struck in 627; but the best known and the most finely executed are the flat copper and silver pieces (Pl. VI, 5) which bear the name *Napkī Malik* ; but whether this prince was a Persian or a Hun is doubtful.

These Sassanian coins were the prototypes of degenerate base silver pieces which are found in large quantities throughout Rājputāna, and must have served as currency for the early Rājpūt states there for centuries. At first they preserve the thin flat fabric of their models (Pl. VI, 6), but as the head on the obverse and the fire-altar on the reverse become more debased they grow thicker and more dumpy. The curious coins known as *Gadhiya Paisa* (Pl. VI, 8), which circulated in the same districts and also in Gujarāt, probably down to a later period, also show traces of a Sassanian origin. The silver coins with the legend *Śrīmad Ādivarāha* on the reverse, and Vishṇu in his boar avatar (Varāha) as the type of the obverse, retain traces of a fire-altar below the inscription. These have been attributed to the powerful Bhoja-deva of Kanauj (840-890), whose family, Gurjara in origin, had formerly ruled in south Rājputāna. Very similar in fabric are those inscribed *Śrī Vigraha*, assigned to Vigrahapāla I, circ. A.D. 910, of the Bengal Pāla dynasty.

All these debased coins follow the weight standard of their Sassanian originals, which represented the Attic drachma of 67·5 grains, and in inscriptions they are actually called "*drammas.*"

II. COINS OF THE RĀJPŪT DYNASTIES

The coins of the various Rājpūt princes ruling in Hindustān and Central India are usually gold, copper or billon, very rarely silver. The gold coins are all "*drammas*" in weight ; the usual type, which appears to have been struck first by Gāṅgeya-deva Vikramāditya (1015-1040) of the Kalachuri dynasty of Ḍahāla (Jabalpūr), bears the familiar goddess (Lakshmī) on the obverse (Pl. VI, 10), with a slight deviation from the Gupta device, in that the goddess has four instead of two arms ; on the reverse is an inscription giving the king's name in old Nāgarī (Fig. 5). Of the same type are the gold coins of six Chandel kings of Mahoba (Pl. VI, 9) in Bundelkhand (circ. 1055-1280), of the Tomara dynasty of Ajmer and Dehlī (978-1128), and of the Rāṭhor kings of Kanauj (1080-1193). On the conquest of Kanauj, Muḥammad of Ghor actually struck a few gold pieces in this style. On the gold of the last three princes of the Kalachuri dynasty of Mahākośala, in the Central Provinces (circ. 1060-1140), a rampant lion is substituted for the seated goddess on the obverse.

The seated bull and horseman, the almost invariable devices on Rājpūt copper and billon coins, were introduced by the Brahman kings of Gandhāra, or Ohind (circ. 860-950), who first used them on silver; the commonest of these are the issues of Spalapati-deva (Pl.VI, 12) and Samanta-deva. The later coins of the dynasty, however, degenerate into billon. The name of the king in Nāgarī appears along with the bull on the reverse, and on the obverse of the Ohind coins is an inscription hitherto undeciphered, but probably in some Turanian script. Bull and Horseman coins, either copper or billon, were also struck by the Tomara and Chauhan dynasties of Dehlī (Pl.VI,11), the Rāṭhors of Kanauj, Amṛitapāla Rāja of Budāyūn (Budāon), and the Rājpūt kings of Narwar (1220-1260; Pl. VI, 13). Some of these last, in imitation of the Muḥammadan invaders, placed dates in the Vikrama era[1] on their coins. The Narwar horseman on later coins is particularly crude in design. The Mahārājas of Kāngra continued to strike degenerate Bull and Horseman coins, from 1315 down to 1625. Deviations from this conventional type are rare. There is a unique coin of Śrī Kamara, king of Ohind, with a lion on the obverse and a peacock on the reverse, while three kings of the same dynasty issued copper with an elephant obverse and a lion reverse.

A few copper coins of the Mahākośala kings and of Jayavarma of Mahoba have a figure of Hanuman on the obverse and a Nāgarī legend on the reverse; and a

[1] The Vikrama era starts in 58 B.C. (See page 24 ante.)

similar legend takes the place of the bull on some copper pieces of Asalla-deva and Gaṇapati-deva of Narwar.

III. THE COINAGE OF KASHMĪR

The early history of Kashmīr as an independent kingdom is obscure; trustworthy annals do not begin till its conquest by Mihiragula in the sixth century. From that time down till about 1334, when it was conquered by the Muhammadans, the country was ruled by four successive dynasties. The earliest coins are considered to be those with the head of a king on the obverse and a vase on the reverse, attributed from the inscription *Khiṅgi* to a certain Khiṅgila of the fifth century. A number of coins of the eighth century, struck by princes of the Nāga dynasty, are known: these are for the most part of very base gold, and were imitated from the standing king and seated goddess issues of the Little Yueh-chi, who, as we have seen, conquered Kashmīr about the year 475, and the name of the original leader of that tribe, *Kidāra*, still appears written vertically under the king's arm. The workmanship of these degenerate pieces (Pl. VI, 16) is of the rudest, and the devices would be quite unintelligible without a knowledge of their antecedents. Some copper coins give the name Toramāṇa, but the identification of this prince with the famous Hūṇa chief presents many difficulties.

With the accession of Śaṅkara Varma, the first of the Varma dynasty, in A.D. 833, gold practically disappears. From the middle of the ninth century nearly all the kings whose names are recorded in Kalhaṇa's great chronicle history of Kashmīr, the *Rājataraṅgiṇī*, of the twelfth century, are represented by copper coins, but the uniform degradation of the fabric deprives them of all interest. Among these are the coins of two queens, Sugandhā and Diddā (980-1003) (Pl. VI, 15), the latter chiefly remarkable for an adventurous career. The flourishing state of sculpture and architecture during the eighth and ninth centuries, and the natural artistic skill of the Kashmīrī people, suggest that this extreme debasement of the coinage may at least be due as much to a conservative dislike and suspicion of innovation as to a lack of cunning in the engravers. Many parallels could be cited, the classical example being the Attic tetradrachm, the archaic style of which continued unchanged at Athens even during the brilliant age of Pheidias.

The one break in this monotonous Kashmīrī series occurs in the reign of the tyrant Harsha-deva (1089-1111), who struck both gold and silver in imitation of the ornate gold of Koṅgudeśa (Pl. VII, 5) in Southern India, with an elephant's head on the obverse. The same king also issued a gold coin with a Horseman obverse and the usual seated goddess on the reverse (Pl. VI, 14).

The sparseness and inferiority of the coinage during the period under discussion in this chapter must be attributed chiefly to the general insecurity, caused by the continual quarrels between the numerous petty states. This state of unrest, together with the previous impoverishment of the country at the hands of the Huns, doubtless accounts for the small output of gold. It must be remembered that mercantile contracts in India have always been carried on largely by notes of hand (*hundīs*), and in times of disturbance these could be conveyed more safely from city to city than coined money.

The scarcity of silver was due to other causes. At this period the world supply of this metal seems to have been drawn chiefly from Central Asia. The rise of the Arab power and the consequent disturbances in Central Asia interrupted trade between India and the west by land and sea, and must have curtailed, if they did not cut off completely, the import of silver from abroad. So we find the Rājpūt states reduced to employing an alloy, billon, which was almost certainly used by them as a substitute for the more precious metal.

It is a most illuminating fact that gold, formerly exported from India, disappears from the coinage of Europe at about this very period, while silver is reduced to the meagre Carolingian *penny* standard.

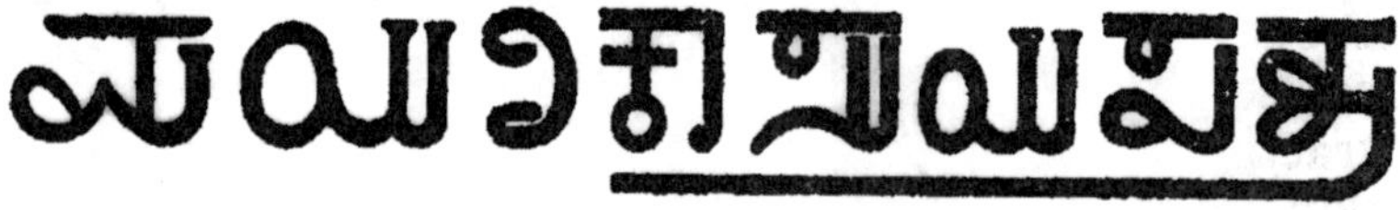

Fig. 6. Kanarese Script : *Mayili kāsu ippatu*, "A token of 20 cash."

VI

THE COINAGE OF SOUTHERN INDIA

The difficulties of the historian in tracing the fortunes of the numerous clans and dynasties which contended for sovereignty in the south from the third to the fourteenth century have been enumerated by Vincent Smith in his *Oxford History of India*. Even fewer guide-posts mark the path of the numismatist. Legends on South Indian coins are rare, and, when they occur are short, giving simply the ruler's name or title : dates are rarer still. As in the early coinage of the Greeks, the heraldic symbol or cognizance serves as the stamp of authority ; the fish, for example, is so used by the rulers of the Pāṇḍya dynasty. But in India we receive little help from contemporary records; and the habit, which conquerors indulged, of incorporating on their issues the cognizance of vanquished peoples, and the extensive imitation of popular and well-established types, worse confounds the confusion. In assigning coins to dynasties reliance has often to be placed upon the evidence of find-spots, a dubious method at all times, but least unsatisfactory for copper, which seldom circulates freely beyond the country of its origin. Again, the isolation of the southern peninsula is as marked in the development of the coinage as in political history. With the sole exception of the elephant pagodas of the Gajapati dynasty, imitated by Harsha-deva of Kashmīr, there is no certain point of contact between the south and the north after the third century A.D. Finally, the currency of the south has not received that attention from scholars which has been bestowed upon the more attractive money of the north. A careful systematic study, in conjunction with the historical material now available, would doubtless throw considerable light upon it and its strikers.

Certain marked characteristics belong to the coinage of the south, which, in spite of foreign irruptions and their consequent innovations, have persisted until recent times. Gold and copper were the metals used almost exclusively; of the former there were two denominations, the *hūn*, *varāha* or *pagoda*[1] (50 to 60 grains) and the *fanam* (five to six grains), based respectively on the weights of two seeds, the *kaḷanju* or molucca bean (*Cæsalpina bonduc*) and the *mañjāḍi* (*Adenathera pavonina*). Copper coins were called *kāsu*, of which the English corruption is "cash," while the rare silver coins appear to have followed the gold standard. The Travancore silver *chakram* was equal in weight to the fanam. The gold coin had an independent development in the south, the various stages of which can be marked. The earliest specimens—the age of these is doubtful—are spherules of plain gold with a minute punch-mark on one side (Pl. VII, 1); these developed into the cup-shaped "padma-ṭaṅkas," stamped with punches, first on one side only, later on both obverse and reverse. Finally came die-struck pieces, of which the small thick Vijayanagar pagodas are the typical southern form. Another characteristic is the preference for tiny coins: this is particularly evident from about the sixteenth century, when copper coins tend to decrease in size, and

[1] *Hūn* is a Hindustānī corruption of *honnu*, Kanarese for "a half pagoda"; *Varāha* is probably derived from the boar (varāha) cognizance on Eastern Chālukya coins; the origin of *Pagoda*, as introduced by the Portugese and applied to this coin, is obscure, cf. Yule and Burnell, *Hobson-Jobson* under "Pagoda." The considerable variation in the weight of the pagodas issued by different dynasties may be due simply to different local standards; but if the Chālukyas were, as is supposed, of Gurjara origin, the heavier weights of their coins may reflect the influence of the "dramma."

the fanam acquired a wide popularity; the silver *tārēs* of Kalikat (Calicut), which weigh only one or two grains, must be the smallest known currency.[1] A great variety of devices and symbols, usually Hindu gods and emblems, also characterizes the copper currency, especially after the fifteenth century, and this feature adds considerably to the difficulty of correct attribution.

The dynasties of the south may be divided into two territorial groups—(1) the kingdoms of the Deccan—all the country between the river Narbadā on the north and the Kṛishṇa and Tuṅgabhadrā on the south—and the Mysore country; Telugu was the language of the former, Kanarese of the latter. (2) The remainder of the peninsula, where Tamil and its cognate dialects were spoken, the country of the Pāṇḍyas, Cheras, Choḷas, Pallavas and their successors.

During the first two centuries of the Christian era, and even after the disappearance of the silver punch-marked coins, perhaps about A.D. 200, the currency of the south consisted chiefly of imported Roman gold[2] along with the spherules already mentioned. A certain quantity of Roman silver must also have been in circulation, while the small copper pieces bearing Roman devices and legends—one of them seems to give the name of the Emperor Theodosius (A.D. 393)—were probably local productions.

Conjecture has assigned the earliest coins connected with a local dynasty to the Kurumbas, a pastoral tribe inhabiting the present Arcot district. One type of these copper pieces with a two-masted ship on the obverse is evidently derived from the similar Andhra issues struck for the Coromandel coast, and so may belong to the third century A.D.

[1] The silver *hemitetartemoria* of Athens weighed 1·4 grs. each.

[2] In 1850 a large number of Roman aurei, amounting, it is said, to five coolie loads, were unearthed near Kannanur: most emperors between Augustus, 29 B C., and Antoninus Pius, A.D. 161, were represented. Cf. "Remarks on Some Lately Discovered Roman Coins," *J.A.S.B.*, 1851, p. 371.

I. COINAGE OF THE DECCAN AND MYSORE

The first great dynasty to dominate Southern India was that of the Chālukyas (a foreign tribe probably of Hūṇa-Gurjara origin), founded by Pulakeśin I in the middle of the sixth century, whose capital was at Bādāmī in the Bījāpūr district. His grandson, Pulakeśin II (A.D. 608-642), became paramount in the Deccan, but the kingdom was overthrown by the Rāshṭrakūṭas in 753. In 973, however, a Chālukya prince, Tailapa, retrieved the fortunes of his family and founded the Western Chālukya kingdom with its capital at Kalyāṇi, and this lasted till 1190, after which the Chālukyas of the west, overthrown by the Hoysaḷas, became petty chiefs. Meanwhile, in the middle of the seventh century another dynasty, known as the Eastern Chālukyas, had been established by Vishṇuvardhana, brother of the great Pulakeśin II, in Kaliṅga with its capital at Veṅgī, which lasted till the eleventh century, when it was overthrown by the Choḷas.

The earliest coin assignable to a Chālukya prince is a base silver piece of Vishṇuvardhana (615-633), with a lion device and the king's title in Telugu, *Vishama-siddhi*, "Successful in scaling the inaccessible places," on the obverse, and a trident flanked by two lamps on the reverse. Certain pagodas, fanams and copper coins, perhaps of an earlier date, from the appearance on them of the boar, the cognizance of the Chālukyas, have been conjectured to belong to that dynasty. To the Eastern Chālukya princes, Śaktivarman (1000-1012) and Rājarāja (1012-1062), belong large flat gold pieces, also depicting the boar symbol, but with blank reverses (Pl. VII, 4).

The curious cup-shaped "padma-ṭaṅkas" (lotus ṭaṅkas) were possibly first struck by the Kadambas (Pl. VII, 2), inhabiting Mysore and Kanara. Similar coins, but with a lion or a temple in place of the lotus and legends in old Kanarese, were struck by the Western Chālukya kings, Jayasiṁha, Jagadekamalla and Trailokyamalla, of the eleventh and twelfth centuries. In 1913, 16,586 of these cup-shaped coins were unearthed at Kodur in the Nellore district, and this find shows that the type was subsequently adopted by the Telugu-Choḷa chiefs of the Nellore district in the thirteenth century.

The Hoysaḷa chiefs, who rose to paramount power under Ballāḷa II on the ruins of the Western Chālukya kingdom, had for their cognizance a maned lion. Some heavy gold coins with old Kanarese legends, which bear that emblem, have, therefore, with probability been assigned to them. On one of these appears the interesting inscription, *Śrī Taḷakāḍa gonda*, "He who took the glorious Taḷkāḍ," the capital of the old Koṅgu-Chera kingdom.

There are numerous South Indian coins belonging to the twelfth century which afford no certain clue to their strikers. Among these the following have been tentatively assigned to petty dynasties who succeeded to the territories of the Chālukyas: to the Kākatīya or Gaṇapati dynasty of Waraṅgal (1110-1323), pagodas, fanams and copper coins with a couchant bull on the obverse and incomplete Nāgarī legends on the reverse; to Someśvara, one of the Kalachuri chiefs of Kalyāṇa (1162-1175), pagodas and fanams with the king's titles in old Kanarese on the reverse, and on the obverse a figure advancing to the right; to the Yādavas of Devagiri (1187-1311), a pagoda and a silver coin, bearing a kneeling figure of Garuḍa on the obverse.

There remain to be noticed the coins of three dynasties. The original home of the Gajapatis, "Elephant-Lords," was Koṅgudesa—Western Mysore with the modern districts of Coimbatore and Salem. About the ninth century these Chera kings fled before the invading Choḷas to Orissa, and there were coined the famous "Elephant pagodas" (Pl. VII, 5) and fanams, which Harsha-deva of Kashmīr (A.D. 1089) copied. The scroll device on the reverse also appears on some of the anonymous boar pagodas attributed to the Chālukyas. To Anantavarman Choḍagaṅga, a member of that branch of the Gaṅga dynasty of Mysore who settled in Kaliṅga

(Orissa), and ruled there from the sixth to the eleventh century, are assigned fanams with a recumbent bull, conch and crescent on the obverse, and Telugu regnal dates on the reverse. The gold coins of two of the later Kādamba chiefs of Goa, Vishṇu Chittadeva (circ. 1147) and Jayakeśin III (circ. 1187), are also known; these bear the special Kādamba symbol, the lion passant on the obverse, and a Nāgarī legend on the reverse. One interesting inscription of the latter runs as follows: "The brave Jayakeśideva, the destroyer of the Mālavas who obtained boons from the holy Saptakoṭīsa (*i.e.* Śiva)."

II. THE COINAGE OF TAMIL STATES

The Tamil states of the far south first became wealthy owing to their foreign sea-borne trade. Tradition has defined with some exactness the territories held by the three principal races in ancient times; the Pāṇḍyas inhabited the modern Madura and Tinnevelly districts, the Choḷas the Coromandel Coast (Choḷamandalam), and the Chera or Keraḷa country comprised the district of Malabar together with the states of Cochin and Travancore. Although their frontiers varied considerably at different periods, this distribution is sufficiently accurate for a study of their coin types.

Nevertheless history affords but few glimpses in early times of these peoples: the Pallavas, as is evident from inscriptions, a native pastoral tribe akin to the Kurumbas, were the first dominant power in the extreme south. At first Buddhists, but later converted to Brahmanical Hinduism, during the sixth, seventh and eighth centuries they extended their territories from their capital, Kāñchī, the modern Conjeeveram, until these included even Ceylon; but they suffered considerably from wars with the Chālukyas, and were overwhelmed in the ninth century by the Choḷas and Pāṇḍyas. It was under the patronage of the Pallavas that South Indian architecture and sculpture began in the sixth century. The earlier Pallava coins, a legacy from the Andhras, are indistinguishable from those of the Kurumbas; later pagodas and fanams bear the Pallava emblem, the maned lion, either on obverse or reverse (Pl. VII, 8),[1] but the legends remain undeciphered.

The Pāṇḍyas had a chequered career: at first independent, then subject to the Pallavas, they emerge in the ninth century to fall once more during the eleventh and twelfth centuries under the domination of the Choḷas. In the thirteenth century they were the leading Tamil state, but gradually sank into local chieftains. The earliest Pāṇḍya coins retain the ancient square form, but are die-struck, with an elephant on the obverse and a blank reverse; later coins have a peculiar angular device on the reverse; others of a still later period display a diversity of emblems, such as wheels, scrolls and crosses. The Pāṇḍya coins, assigned to a period from the seventh to the tenth century, are gold and copper, and all bear the fish emblem adopted by the later chiefs (Pl. VII, 3): the innovation is supposed to mark a change in religion from Buddhism to Brahmanism. The fish appears sometimes singly, sometimes in pairs, and sometimes, especially on the later copper coins, in conjunction with other symbols, particularly the Choḷa standing figure and the Chālukyan boar. The inscriptions on these, such as *Soṇādu koṇḍān*, "He who conquered the Choḷa country," and *Ellān-talaiy-āṇān*, "He who is chief of the world," are in Tamil, but the intermingling of the symbols, evident marks of conquest, makes any certain attribution difficult.

Madura, the later capital of the Pāṇḍyas, was captured by 'Alāu-d-dīn in 1311, and an independent Muhammadan dynasty ruled there from 1334 to 1377, after which it was added to the Vijayanagar kingdom.

The Choḷas were supreme in Southern India from the accession of Rājarāja the Great in 985 down to 1035, during which period they extended their conquests to the Deccan and subdued Ceylon. After some years

[1] This attribution is somewhat doubtful.

of eclipse they rose again under Rājendra Kulottuṅga I (acc. 1074), who was related to the Eastern Chālukyas of Veṅgī. The Choḷa power declined in the thirteenth century. The earlier coins of the dynasty, before 985, are gold and silver pieces, portraying a tiger seated under a canopy along with the Pāṇḍya fish (Pl. VII, 6); the names inscribed on them have not been satisfactorily explained. The later class of Choḷa coins, all copper, have a standing figure on the obverse and a seated figure on the reverse, with the name *Rāja Rāja* in Nāgarī. This type spread with the Choḷa power, and was slavishly copied by the kings of Ceylon (1153-1296; cf. Pl. VII, 7), and its influence is also noticeable on the earlier issues of the Nāyaka princes of Madura and Tinnevelly.

Only one coin has been attributed to a Chera dynasty. A silver piece in the British Museum, with Nāgarī legends on both sides (Pl. VII, 9), belongs to the Keraḷa country, the extreme southern portion of the western coast, and has been assigned to the eleventh or twelfth century.

III. COINAGE OF THE EMPIRE OF VIJAYANAGAR AND LATER DYNASTIES

The great mediæval kingdom of Vijayanagar was founded in 1336 by five brothers as a bulwark against Muhammadan conquest, and continued to flourish under three successive dynasties until the battle of Tālikota, 1565; the members of a fourth dynasty ruled as minor chiefs at Chandragiri until the end of the seventeenth century.

The small, dumpy pagodas of Vijayanagar, with their half and quarter divisions, set a fashion which has lasted to the present age. Coins, gold or copper, of more than twelve rulers are known: on these appear a number of devices, the commonest being the bull, the elephant, various Hindu deities, and the fabulous "gaṇḍabheruṇḍa," a double eagle holding an elephant in each beak and claw. A pagoda on which a god and goddess appear sitting side by side (Pl. VII, 12) was struck both by

Harihara I (acc. 1336) and Devarāya.[1] The great Kṛishṇarāya, during whose reign (1509-1529) the Empire was at its height, was evidently a devotee of Vishṇu. He struck the popular "Durgi pagoda,"[2] on which that god is portrayed holding the discus and conch (Pl. VII, 11). Other coins of the dynasty which acquired fame were the "Gandikata pagoda" of Rāmarāya (d. 1565), which had a figure of Vishṇu standing under a canopy on the obverse; and the "Veṅkaṭapati pagoda," struck by one of the rajas, named Veṅkaṭa, of the fourth dynasty. On the obverse of this coin Vishṇu is standing under an arch, and on the reverse is the Nāgarī legend, *Śrī Veṅkaṭeśvarāya namaḥ*, "Adoration to the blessed Veṅkaṭeśvara," Veṅkaṭeśvara being the deity of Veṅkaṭādri, a sacred hill near Chandragiri. The so-called "three swami pagoda," introduced by Tirumalarāya (circ. 1570), displays three figures, the central one standing, the other two seated. These are said to be either Lakshmana with Rāma and Sīta, or Veṅkaṭeśvara with his two wives. The legends on Vijayanagar coins are either in Kanarese or Nāgarī; the latter is most commonly used, by the later kings exclusively.

During the sixteenth and seventeenth centuries the Nāyaka princes of Tanjore, Madura and Tinnevelly and the Setupatis of Rāmnāḍ, originally in subjection to Vijayanagar, gradually assumed independence. The earlier coinage of the Madura Nāyakas bears the names of the chiefs on the reverse in Tamil, but their later coins were struck in the name of Veṅkaṭa, the "pageant" sovereign of Vijayanagar. Somewhat later, probably, begin series of copper coins both of Madura and Tinnevelly, with the Telugu legend *Śrī Vīra* on the reverse and a multitude of varying devices on the obverse; these include the gods Hanuman and Ganesh, human

[1] The attributes of the two seated figures are sometimes those of Śiva, sometimes those of Vishṇu; there is some difficulty in distinguishing between the coins of Devarāya I (1406-1410) and Devarāya II (1421-1445).

[2] Durgi = belonging to durga, a hill fort. The coins are said to have been struck at Chitaldrūg.

figures, the elephant, bull, lion, a star, the sun and moon, etc. A similar copper series, with double or single crossed lines on the reverse, are found in large quantities in Mysore. Yet another series with the same reverse, also found in Mysore, bears on the obverse the Kanarese numerals from 1 to 31.

With the extinction of the Vijayanagar kingdom the number of petty states minting their own money rapidly increased. For example, the "Durgi pagoda" continued to be struck by the Nāyakas of Chitaldrūg from 1689 to 1779; the god and goddess type was continued by the Nāyakas of Ikkeri (1559-1640), and later on at Bednūr (1640-1763). On the conquest of the latter city in 1763 by Ḥaidar ʿAlī, the type was for a short time struck by him with addition of the initial letter of his name "hē" on the reverse; but this initial soon became the obverse and the year and date in Persian occupied the reverse. So also the East India Company issued, from Madras, pagodas of the "three swami" type, and both British and Dutch Companies struck "Veṅkaṭapati pagodas," but with a granulated reverse. These latter Company coins acquired the name "Porto Novo pagodas," from one of their places of issue. The famous "Star pagoda" was of this type, with the addition of a star on the reverse. Likewise the Niẓāms of Ḥaidarābād and the Nawābs of the Karnatic struck pagodas of various types, those of the Nawāb Ṣafdar ʿAlī are of the "Porto Novo" type with an "ʿAin" on the granulated reverse.

At Bālāpūr, Qolār (Kolār), Gūtī and Ooscotta were struck fanams, and at Imtiyāzgarh pagodas, with Persian inscriptions in the name of the Mughal Emperor, Muḥammad Shāh, and a small copper coinage in the name of ʿĀlamgīr II was in general circulation in parts of the peninsula; small silver coins of a similar type are also known. An exceedingly interesting fanam, as well as some copper pieces, bear the Nāgarī legend, *Śrī Rājā Śiva* on the obverse, and *Chhatrapati*, "Lord of the umbrella," on the reverse, and have with great probability been assigned to the great Marāṭhā chief, Śivajī.

The coinage of the old Keraḷa country, the Malabar coast, was, in 1657, the Portugese Viaggio di Vincenzo Maria informs us, in the hands of the rulers of four states, Kannanur, Kalikat, Cochin and Travancore. It is distinguished from that of the rest of the peninsula by its large employment of silver, the most remarkable among these silver coins being the *tārēs*, said to have been struck in Kalikat, which have a *śaṅkha* shell on the obverse and a deity on the reverse, and weigh only from one to two grains each. The same device, a *śaṅkha* shell, appears on the silver *puttans* of Cochin, struck both by the Dutch and the native rulers, and also on the old and modern silver *vellis* of Travancore. Various gold fanams were current in Travancore before the nineteenth century, the oldest, known as the *rasi*, also has a *śaṅkha* on the obverse, and is closely allied to the "Vīra rāya" fanams of Kalikat. During the eighteenth century the copper coinage of Travancore was known as the "Anantan kāsu"; on the obverse was a five-headed cobra, and on the reverse the value of the coin, one, two, four or eight "cash" written in Tamil. In the years 1764 and 1774 the Moplah chief of Kannanur, 'Alī Rāja, struck double silver and gold fanams with Persian inscriptions, recording his name and the date (Pl. VII, 13). The Muhammadan coinage of Mysore is reserved for a later chapter.

Fig. 7. The Kalima in ornate Arabic script on early tankah of Altamsh.

VII

THE MUHAMMADAN DYNASTIES OF DEHLĪ

IN earlier chapters we have seen how the Greek, the Śaka, the Pahlava and the Kushāṇa invader each in his turn modified the contemporary coinage of Northern India; the conquests of Muḥammad Ghorī wrought a revolution. The earlier Muhammadan rulers, it is true, conceded so much to local sentiment as to reproduce for a time the Bull and Horseman issues of the Rājpūt states, and even to inscribe their names and titles thereon in the Nāgarī script, but there was no real or lasting compromise; the coinage was too closely bound up with the history and traditions of their religion Their issues in India are the lineal descendants of those of earlier Muhammadan dynasties in Central Asia and elsewhere. The engraving of images was forbidden by the Faith; and accordingly, with some notable exceptions, pictorial devices cease to appear on Indian coins. Both obverse and reverse are henceforth entirely devoted to the inscription, setting forth the king's name and titles as well as the date, in the Hijrī era,[1] and place of striking or mint, now making their first appearance on Indian money. The inscribing of the sovereign's name on the coinage was invested with special importance in the eyes of the Muslim world, for this

[1] The first year of the Hijrī era begins on Friday, July 15th-16th, A.D. 622.

privilege, with the reading of his name in the *khutba*, or public prayer, were actions implying the definite assumption of regal power. Another new feature was the inclusion in the inscription of religious formulæ, that most commonly used being the Kalima or profession of faith. "*There is no god but Al ah, and Muḥammad is the prophet of Allah.*" This practice, followed by many subsequent Muhammadan rulers in India, owed its origin to the crusading zeal of the early Khalifs of Syria in the eighth century.

The fabric of the coinage thus underwent a complete transformation; not all at once, but gradually, as new districts were subjected to Muhammadan conquerors, money of the new type spread over the whole peninsula except the extreme south. Yet owing, no doubt, to its sectarian association, it was not, until the great Mughal currency had attained a position of predominating importance, voluntarily imitated by independent communities.

The Muhammadans were also destined to set up a new standard of weight, but before this was accomplished nearly five centuries were to elapse. The period under discussion in this chapter is chiefly interesting for the reappearance of silver in the currency, due to the reopening of commercial relations with Central Asia, and for the successive attempts made by various sovereigns to restore order out of the chaos into which the coinage had fallen during the preceding centuries. The gold and silver currency was rectified by Altamsh and his successors with little difficulty; but the employment of billon for their smaller money was fatal; for the mixture of silver and copper in varying proportions,[1] so liable to abuse, proved in the end unworkable as a circulating medium; and not until Sher Shāh substituted pure copper for billon, and adjusted this to his new standard

[1] The variation is due to the fact that silver and copper only form a homogeneous alloy when mixed in the ratio of 71·89 of the former to 28·11 of the latter. This fact was certainly unknown at this period. Cf. *J.A.S.B.*, N.S., XXXV. p. 22, "The Currency of the Pathan Sultans," by H.R. Nevill.

silver coin, the rupee, was the currency established on a firm basis.

The earliest Muhammadan kingdom in India was set up by 'Imādu-d-dīn ibn Qāsim, in Sind, in A.D. 712, but as it exerted little influence on its neighbours, the insignificant coins issued by its later governors need not detain us. The gates of the North-West were first opened to Muslim invaders by the expeditions of the great Sulṭān Maḥmūd of Ghaznī between the years A.D. 1001 and 1026. In 1021 the Panjāb was annexed as a province of his dominions, and after 1051 Lāhor became the capital of the later princes of his line, driven out of Ghaznī by the chieftains of Ghor. Here they struck small billon coins with an Arabic legend in the Cufic[1] script on the reverse, retaining the Rājpūt bull on the obverse. Maḥmūd himself struck a remarkable silver *tankah*[2] at Lāhor, called on the coin *Maḥmūdpūr*, with a reverse inscription in Arabic, and his name and a translation of the Kalima in Sanskrit on the obverse.

The last of these Ghaznavid princes of Lāhor, Khusrū Malik, was deposed in 1187 by Muḥammad bin Sām of Ghor (Mu'izzu-d-dīn of the coins), who, after the final defeat of Pṛithvīrāj of Ajmer and his Hindu allies at the second battle of Thāṇeśar or Tarāin, in 1192, founded the first Muhammadan dynasty of Hindustān, which nevertheless actually starts with his successor, Quṭbu-d-dīn Aibak, the first Sultan to fix his capital at Dehlī. In dealing with the coins of the five successive dynasties who ruled in Dehlī from 1206 to 1526, it will be convenient to recognize three periods: (1) from the accession of Quṭbu-d-dīn Aibak in 1206 to the death of Ghiyāṣu-d-dīn Tughlaq in 1324, (2) the reign of Muḥammad bin Tughlaq 1324-1351, (3) from the accession of Fīroz Shāh III, 1351, to the death of Ibrāhīm Lodī, 1526.

[1] Cufic is the earliest rectilineal form of Arabic script.

[2] Tankah is an Indian name applied to coins of various weights and metals at different periods. For example, to the large silver and gold pieces of Nāṣir-d-dīn Maḥmūd, and later to a special copper issue of the Mughal Akbar.

I. COINS OF THE EARLY SULTANS, A.D. 1206-1324 (A.H. 602-725)

The gold coins which Muḥammad bin Sām struck in imitation of the issues of the Hindu kings of Kanauj with the goddess Lakshmī on the obverse, are, except for the earliest gold issue of Ḥaidar 'Alī of Mysore, without a parallel in Muhammadan history. He apparently struck no silver for his Indian dominions; in fact, two centuries of invasion had so impoverished the country that for forty years the currency consisted almost entirely of copper and billon: hardly any gold appears to have been struck, and silver coins of the earlier Sultans are scarce. The third Sultan, Altamsh[1] (1211-1236), however, issued several types of the silver tankah (Pl. VIII, 2), the earliest of which has a portrait of the king on horseback on the obverse. The latest type bears witness to the diploma of investiture he had received in 1228 from the Khalif of Baghdād, Al-Mustanṣir. The inscriptions run as follows: on the obverse, "*In the reign of the Imām Al-Mustanṣir, the commander of the faithful,*" and on the reverse, "*The mighty Sultan Shamsu-d-dunyā wā-d-dīn, the father of the victorious, Sultan Altamsh.*" Both legends are enclosed in circles, leaving circular margins in which are inscribed the name of the mint and the date in Arabic. This type was followed, sometimes with slight variations, by seven succeeding Sultans, and although the Khalif actually died in 1242, the words, "*in the reign of,*" were not dropped until the time of Ghiyāṣu-d-dīn Balban (1266-1286). Gold, though minted by 'Alāu-d-dīn Mas'ūd, Nāṣiru-d-dīn Maḥmūd, Balban and Jalālu-d-dīn Khiljī, was not common until 'Alāu-d-dīn Muḥammad (1296-1316) had enriched his treasury by conquests in Southern India. These gold coins (Pl. VIII, 5) are replicas of the silver in weight and design. Divisional pieces of the silver tankah are extremely rare. 'Alāu-d-dīn, whose silver issues are

[1] The correct form of the Sultan's name is Iltutmish; Altamsh is a popular corruption.

very plentiful, changed the design by dropping the name of the Khalif from the obverse and substituting the self-laudatory titles, "*The second Alexander, the right hand of the Khalifate*"; at the same time he confined the marginal inscription to the obverse. His successor, Quṭbu-d-dīn Mubārak, whose issues are in some respects the finest of the whole series, employed the old Indian square shape[1] for some of his gold, silver and billon. On his coins appear the even more arrogant titles, "*The supreme head of Islām, the Khalif of the Lord of heaven and earth.*" Ghiyāṣu-d-dīn Tughlaq was the first Indian sovereign to use the title *Ghāzī*, "Champion of the faith."

Among the greatest rarities of this period are the silver tankahs of two *rois faineants*, Shamsu-d-dīn Kaiyūmarṣ, the infant son of Mu'izzu-d-dīn Kaiqubād (1287-1290), and Shihābu-d-dīn 'Umar, brother of Quṭbu-d-dīn Mubārak, who each occupied the throne only a few months.

Most of the coins struck in billon by these early Sultans, including Muḥammad of Ghor, are practically uniform in size and weight (about 56 grains), the difference in value depending upon the proportions in which the two metals were mixed in them. This question has not yet been fully investigated, but it is probable that different denominations were marked by different types.[2] The drawback to such a coinage lay, as already noted, in the impossibility of obtaining uniformity in coins of the same denomination, and in the consequent liability to abuse. Numerous varieties were struck. The Indian type known as the *Dehlīwāla*, with the humped bull and the sovereign's name in Nāgarī on the reverse, and the Dehlī Chauhan type of horseman on the obverse, lasted till the reign of 'Alāu-d-dīn Mas'ūd (1241-1246); on some coins of this class Altamsh's name is associated with that of Chāhada-deva

[1] Two gold coins of 'Alāu-d-dīn Muḥammad are the earliest known Muhammadan coins of this shape. Cf. *Num. Chron.*, 1921, p. 345.

[2] *J.A.S.B.*, N.S., XXXV, p. 25.

of Narwar. Another type, with the Horseman obverse and the Sultan's name and titles in Arabic on the reverse (Pl. VII, 3), survived till Nāṣiru-d-dīn Maḥmūd's reign,[1] when it was replaced by coins with a similar reverse, but, on the obverse, the king's name in Arabic appears in a circle surrounded by his titles in Nāgarī (Pl. VIII, 4). On the commonest type of the later Sultans Arabic legends are in parallel lines on both obverse and reverse. The billon coins of 'Alāu-d-dīn Muḥammad are the first to bear dates. Quṭbu-d-dīn Mubārak employs a number of special types, including those square in shape (Pl. VIII, 6). Billon coins, mostly of the Bull and Horseman type, were also struck by a number of foreigners who invaded Western India during the thirteenth century. The most important of these was the fugitive king of Khwārizm Jalālu-d-dīn Mang-barnī.

The earliest copper of this period is small and insignificant. Some coins, as well as a few billon pieces, bear the inscription *'adl*, which may mean simply "legal," *i.e.* currency (Pl. VIII, 1). Balban introduced a type with the Sultan's name and titles divided between obverse and reverse. All copper is dateless.

The mint names inscribed on the coins of these Sultans sometimes afford valuable historical evidence of the extent of their dominions The general term, *Bilādu-l-hind*, "The Cities of Hind," is the first to appear, on the silver of Altamsh. *Dehlī* is found on the same king's billon and copper. *Lakhnautī*, the modern Gaur in Bengal, also occurs for the first time during this reign; *Sulṭānpūr*, a town on the Beas in the Panjāb, on a silver tankah of Balban; *Dāru-l-islām*, "The seat of Islam" (possibly an ecclesiastical mint in old Dehlī); and *Qila Deogīr* on the gold and silver of 'Alāu-d-dīn Muḥammad; while Quṭbābād is probably Quṭbu-d-dīn Mubārak's designation for Deogīr.

[1] A single specimen is known of the reign of Balban.

II. THE COINAGE OF MUḤAMMAD BIN TUGHLAQ, A.D. 1325-1351 (A.H. 725-752)

Fakhru-d-dīn Jūna, on his coins simply Muḥammad bin Tughlaq, son and murderer of Ghiyāṣu-d-dīn Tughlaq, has not unjustly been called by Thomas "The Prince of moneyers." Not only do his coins surpass those of his predecessors in execution and especially in calligraphy,[1] but his large output of gold, the number of his issues of all denominations, the interest of the inscriptions, reflecting his character and activities, his experiments with the coinage, particularly his forced currency, entitle him to a place among the greatest moneyers of history. For his earliest gold and silver pieces he retained the old 172·8 grain standard of his predecessors. His first experiment was to add to these, in the first year of his reign, gold *dīnars* of 201·6 grains (Pl. VIII, 7) and silver *'adlīs* of 144 grains weight, an innovation aimed apparently at adjusting the coinage to the actual commercial value of the two metals, which had changed with the influx of gold into Northern India after the Sultan's successful campaigns in the Deccan. But the experiment evidently did not work; for after the seventh year of the reign these two new pieces were discontinued.

Muḥammad bin Tughlaq's gold and silver issues, like those of his predecessors, are identical in type. One of the earliest and most curious of these was struck both at Dehlī and Daulatābād (Deogīr), his southern capital, in memory of his father. It bears the superscription of Ghiyāṣu-d-dīn accompanied by the additional title, strange considering the circumstances of his death, *Al Shahīd*, "The Martyr." His staunch orthodoxy is reflected on nearly all his coins, not only in the reappearance of the Kalima, but in the assumption by

[1] The fine calligraphy, however, caused the coin to be reduced in size: all succeeding Sultans reproduced these small thick gold and silver pieces, but not the fine script, with the unfortunate result that the mint name which appears in the margin is frequently missing.

the monarch of such titles as "*The warrior in the cause of God*" and "*The truster in the support of the Compassionate,*" while the names of the four orthodox Khalifs, Abūbakr, 'Umr, 'Uṣmān and 'Alī now appear for the first time on the coinage of India. The early gold and silver, of which about half-a-dozen different types exist, were minted at Dehlī, Lakhnautī, Satgāon, Sulṭānpūr (Warangal), Dāru-l-islām, Tughlaqpūr (Tirhut), Daulatābād, and Mulk-i-Tilang. In A.H. 741 (1340) Muḥammad sent an emissary to the Abbassid Khalif at Cairo for a diploma of investiture, and in the meantime substituted the name of the Khalif Al Mustakfī Billah for his own on the coinage; on the return of the emissary, however, it was discovered that that Khalif had actually died in A.H. 740, so during the latter years of the reign the name of his successor, Al Ḥākim, appeared in its place (Pl. VIII, 8).

At least twenty-five varieties of Muḥammad bin Tughlaq's billon coinage are known. From inscriptions on the Forced Currency, which included tokens representing these billon pieces, we learn the names of their various denominations. There appear to have been two scales of division, one for use at Dehlī, and the other for Daulatābād and the south. In the former the silver tankah was divided into forty-eight, and in the latter into fifty *jaitils*. At Dehlī were current 2-, 6-, 8-, 12- and 16-*ganī* pieces, equal respectively to $\frac{1}{24}$th, $\frac{1}{8}$th, $\frac{1}{6}$th, $\frac{1}{4}$th and $\frac{1}{3}$rd of a tankah. At Daulatābād there were halves (25 *ganī*) and fifths (10 *ganī*). The assignation of their respective values to the actual coins is, however, still a matter of difficulty.[1]

Billon as well as pure copper coins of the later years of the reign bear the names of the two Khalifs. About twelve types[2] of copper money were minted, most of them small and without special interest. Between the years A.H. 730-732 (1329-1332) the

[1] I am indebted to Colonel H. R. Nevill and Mr. H. N. Wright for this information.

[2] Excluding the Forced Currency types.

Sultan attempted to substitute brass and copper tokens (Pl. VIII, 9) for the silver and billon coinage. In order to secure the success of this experiment, he caused such appeals as the following to be inscribed on them: "*He who obeys the Sultan obeys the Compassionate*"; and it is significant that one of these tokens bears an inscription in Nāgarī, the sole example of the use of this script by the orthodox Sultan. These coins were struck at seven different mints, including Dhār in Mālwā, but the scheme was doomed because of the ease with which forgeries were fabricated; they were made in thousands; the promulgation of the edict which accompanied the issue "turned the house of every Hindu into a mint," says a contemporary historian. The Sultan thereupon withdrew the issue, and redeemed geniune and false alike at his own cost.

III. THE COINAGE OF DEHLĪ, FROM 1351 to 1526 (A.H. 752-932)

It has been suggested by historians that the disastrous consequences of Muḥammad bin Tughlaq's experiment with the currency were in part responsible for the disintegration of his wide empire. This is improbable. His successor, Fīroz Shāh Tughlaq, undoubtedly inherited a full treasury, as the vast constructional works he undertook during the thirty-seven peaceful years of his reign prove. But he was no soldier; and the governors of the wealthy Deccan province probably experienced little interference from the distant Court at Dehlī. Daulatābād was an almost impregnable fort, and, doubtless, well stored with munitions. Consequently truculent Viceroys had the sinews of rebellion ready to their hand. The temptation was too great to be resisted. Other governors followed the lead given in the Deccan; the finest provinces rapidly fell away during the disturbed rule of Fīroz's successors and became independent kingdoms; so that in a few years the dominions of the Dehlī kings were reduced to little more than the district round the city,

Their discomfiture was completed when, in 1398, the plundering hosts of Tīmūr swept down through Hindustān and occupied the capital. Under these conditions the coinage naturally degenerated.

The gold of Fīroz Shāh is fairly common, and six types are known. Following his predecessor's example, he inscribed the name of the Khalif Abū-l-'abbās and those of his two successors, Abū-l-fatḥ and 'Abdullah, on the obverse, and his own name on the reverse, accompanied by such titles as "*The right hand of the commander of the faithful*" (*i.e.* the Khalif) and "*The deputy of the commander.*" The latter appears on either the copper or billon coins of nearly every subsequent ruler until Bahlol Lodī's reign. In A.H. 760 (1359) Fīroz associated the name of his son, Fatḥ Khān, with his own on the coinage.

Gold coins of subsequent kings are exceedingly scarce (Pl. VIII, 11); the shortage of silver is even more apparent. Only three silver pieces of Fīroz have ever come to light, and a few are known of Muḥammad bin Fīroz, Maḥmūd Shāh, Muḥammad bin Farīd, Mubārak Shāh II, and 'Ālam Shāh. In the reign of Muḥammad bin Fīroz, the general title, "*The Supreme head of Islām, the commander of the faithful,*" was substituted for the actual name of the Khalif in the inscription. Fīroz Shāh, following the example of Muḥammad bin Tughlaq, issued in large quantities a billon coin of about 144 grains weight (Pl. VIII, 10). This was continued by his successors, but the proportion of silver was apparently gradually reduced. The coinage of the later rulers, though abounding in varieties, is almost confined to copper and billon pieces (Pl. VIII, 12). During the whole period, with but two exceptions, one mint name appears, Dehlī, accompanied by one or other of its honorific titles, *Ḥaẓrat* or *Dāru-l-Mulk*.

The long reign of Fīroz seems to have established his coinage as a popular medium of exchange; and this probably accounts for the prolonged series of his posthumous billon coins, extending over a period of forty years. Some of these and of the posthumous issues of his son,

Muḥammad, and of his grandson, Maḥmūd, were struck by Daulat Khān Lodī and Khiẓr Khān, two sultans who refused to assume the insignia of royalty. The coinage of the Lodī family, Bahlol, Sikandar and Ibrāhīm, despite the difference in standard, bears a close resemblance to that of the Sharqī kings of Jaunpūr. The first and the last minted copper and billon, Sikandar and his son, Maḥmūd, a pretender (1529), billon only. Bahlol (1450-1489) issued a large billon coin, the *Bahlolī*, of about 145 grains (Pl. VIII, 13), and also a copper piece of 140 grains, first introduced by Fīroz, with its half and quarter divisions. The mint name, Dehlī, appears on both Bahlol's and Sikandar's coins, but it is frequently missing from the latter, as the dies were made larger than the coin discs. The name *Shahr Jaunpūr*, "The City Jaunpūr," occurs on the later copper of Bahlol after his reduction of the Sharqī kingdom in 1476. On their billon coins all three kings adopt the formula, "*Trusting in the merciful one*," but on his larger copper pieces Bahlol retained the old, "*Deputy of the commander of the faithful.*" In 1526 Ibrāhīm Lodī was overthrown and killed on the field of Pānīpat by the Mughal Bābur; and once again the fortunes of the Indian coinage changed under the auspices of a foreign dynasty.

Fig. 8. Akbar's Ilāhī formula. Cf. Pl. X, 8 (obverse).

VIII

THE COINAGES OF THE MUHAMMADAN STATES

ALL the states whose coinages form the subject of this chapter, with the exception of Kashmīr, were once provinces subject to the Dehlī Sultans, and owed their independence to the ambition of powerful viceroys, who took advantage at various times of the weakened control of the central power. The earliest issues of each state were more or less close imitations of the Dehlī currency, but local conditions soon introduced modifications in standard and fabric, and in the course of a century each had generally acquired a well-defined and characteristic coinage of its own. Prosperity was usually short-lived; the inevitable period of decay set in; and the coinage, confined at the close to ill-struck copper pieces, illustrates history in striking fashion. Bengal, however, was able to maintain its silver currency to the last.

I. THE COINAGE OF THE GOVERNORS AND SULTANS OF BENGAL

Bengal was brought into subjection to the Dehlī kingdom in 1202 (A.H. 599) by Bakhtiyār Khiljī, who became the first governor of the province. Till 1338 it was nominally ruled from the capital, Lakhnautī, by independent governors; but at least six of these issued coins in their own names; and after 1310 there was a divided governorship, the rulers of East and West Bengal each assuming the right to coin. Independence was gained under one of the rulers of East Bengal, Fakhru-d-dīn Mubārak; and, after a year of discord, Shamsu-d-dīn Ilyās Shāh, in 1339, brought the whole province under his control. From 1339-1358 Bengal was ruled by four dynasties, the house of Ilyās Shāh, 1339-1406 and 1442-1481, the house of the Hindu rāja, Ganesh, 1406-1442, the Ḥabshī kings, 1486-1490, and the house of the greatest of Bengal kings, 'Alāu-d-dīn Ḥusain Shāh, 1493-1538. Bengal was then ruled from Dehlī by Sher Shāh and his family; then independently from 1552-1563 by younger members of his dynasty; and finally by three sovereigns of the Afghān Kararānī family till 1576, when Bengal became a province of Akbar's empire.

Gold coins of Bengal are very scarce, and but one billon coin, of the governor Ghiyāṣu-d-dīn Bahādur (1310-1323) has been found. The place of copper, it is supposed, was supplied by cowries. Silver coins are known of twenty-nine out of the fifty-six governors and sultans, but the silver is inferior in purity to the Dehlī coins; and that of the Sultans is struck to a local standard of 166 grains: they are frequently much disfigured by countermarks and chisel-cuts made by the money-changers. The coins of the governors and Sultans until Shamsu-d-dīn Ilyās Shāh show Dehlī influence in fabric and inscription, and this influence reappears occasionally later. The issues of the earlier governors bear the Kalima on the obverse; for this later governors substitute the name of the last Khalif of Baghdād, Al Must'aṣim. The independent kings adopt various titles expressing their loyalty to the head of Islām, such as "*The right hand of the Khalif, aider of the commander of the faithful*" and "*Succourer of Islām and the Muslims.*" The convert, Jalālu-d-dīn Muḥammad (1414-1431), revived the use of the Kalima, which is continued with two exceptions by all his successors till 'Alāu-d-dīn Ḥusain Shāh's reign. The most usual personal titles are "*The mighty Sultan,*" or "*The strengthened by the support of the Compassionate,*" but certain rulers adopt striking formulæ of their own. Shamsu-d-dīn Ilyās

Shāh, following 'Alāu-d-dīn Muḥammad of Dehlī, called himself "*The Second Alexander*," and Sikandar Shāh (1358-89) was evidently imitating Muḥammad bin Tughlaq in "*The warrior in the cause of the Compassionate.*" One of the most curious and interesting titles appears on a coin of 'Alāu-d-dīn Ḥusain; it runs as follows: "*The Sultan, conqueror over Kāmrū and Kamtah and Jājnagar and Urīssah,*" alluding to his invasions of Assam and Orissa.

The coinage assumes a characteristic local type first under Sikandar (Pl. IX, 1), son of the founder of the house of Ilyās, and henceforth there is much variety of design, the Sultan's name and titles being enclosed in circles, squares, octagons, sometimes with multifoil borders or scalloped edges; margins occur more usually on the reverse only, sometimes on both sides, in which are inscribed the mint and date in Arabic words. Nāṣiru-d-dīn Maḥmūd I (1442-59), abolished the marginal inscription; and from his reign the mint name and date, in figures, appear at the bottom of the reverse area. For some of his coins Jalālu-d-dīn Muḥammad used *Tughra* characters, which, owing to the up-strokes being elongated to the upper edge of the coin, give the curious appearance of a row of organ-pipes. It must be admitted that the majority of Bengal coins are entirely wanting in artistic form, the depths being reached perhaps in some of the issues of Ruknu-d-dīn Bārbak (1459-74); the calligraphy is of the poorest quality; and the Bengali die-cutters frequently reveal their ignorance of Arabic. The fine broad coins of the two Afghān dynasties display an immediate improvement; they are identical in form and inscription with the Dehlī Sūrī coinage, and are struck to Sher Shāh's new silver standard. A special feature of the Bengal coinage is the number of its mints; twenty-one names have been read on the coins, but it is uncertain whether some of these are not temporary names for better-known towns. The most important mints were Lakhnautī, Fīrozābād, Satgāon, Fatḥābād, Ḥusainābād, Naṣratābād and Tānda. Also certain coins are inscribed as struck at "The Mint" and "The Treasury." The broad silver coins of the little state of Jayantāpura, though struck two centuries after the independent coinage of Bengal had disappeared, seem to be a late echo of the popularity it achieved, particularly in the neighbouring hill states.

II. COINAGE OF THE SULTANS OF KASHMĪR[1]

Kashmīr was conquered about the year 1346 by a Swāt, named Shāh Mirzā, who, assuming the title of Shamsu-d-dīn, founded the first Muhammadan dynasty. The most famous of succeeding rulers were the iconoclast Sikandar (1393-1416) and the tolerant Zainu-l-'ābidīn (1420-70). From 1541 to 1551 Kashmīr was ruled by a Mughal governor, Mirzā Ḥaidar, nominally in subjection to the Emperor Humāyūn. In 1561 the Chak dynasty succeeded and ruled till 1589, when Akbar annexed Kashmīr to the empire. Coins are known of sixteen sultans; there are also coins in the local style struck in the names of the Muhgals, Akbar and Humāyūn and of Islām Shāh Sūrī. The gold of these Sultans is extremely scarce, only about twelve specimens being known, including coins of Muḥammad Shāh, Ibrāhīm and Yūsuf. They are all of one type: on the obverse is the Kalima enclosed in a circle, the reverse inscription giving the king's name and titles and the mint, *Kashmīr*, is divided into two parts by a double band running across the face of the coin. Most characteristic of the Kashmīr kingdom are the square silver pieces (Pl. IX, 9); size, shape and design suggest that the model for these may perhaps be found in the recent billon issues of Quṭbu-d-dīn Mubārak of Dehlī (1316-20). Following conservative Kashmīr traditions, the design once fixed remained unchanged till the downfall of the kingdom. The obverse gives the ruler's name accompanied invariably by the title, "*The most mighty*

[1] The chronology of these Sultans, long in doubt, has now been fixed. Cf. *J.R.A.S.*, 1918, p. 451.

Sultan," and the date in figures; on the reverse appears the legend "*Struck in Kashmīr,*" in a square border set diagonally to the sides of the coin, and in the margins the date (usually illegible) in Arabic words. Dates on Kashmīr coins are frequently unreliable, they seem at times to have become conventional along with the style.

The copper coinage follows in general the standard of the preceding Hindu kings and is very poorly executed. In the commonest type the obverse inscription is divided by a bar with a knot in the middle. Zainu-l-'ābidīn struck several kinds of copper; a large crude square type, also found in brass, may belong to an earlier reign. Of Ḥasan Shāh a lead coin has been recorded.

III. COINAGE OF THE SULTANS OF MADURA OR MA'BAR

When Muḥammad bin Tughlaq formed the most southern districts of his kingdom into a province, which he named Ma'bar, he seems to have struck certain types of billon and copper specially for circulation there. In 1334 (A.H. 735) the governor, Jalālu-d-dīn Aḥsan Shāh, proclaimed his independence, and he and his eight successors minted coins of copper and billon[1] in their capital, Madura, until they were subjugated by the king of Vijayanagar in 1371 (A.H. 773). The last coin of 'Alāu-d-dīn Sikandar Shāh is, however, dated A.H. 779. These coins, which are of little interest, follow two types of the Dehlī coinage, one of which has the sultan's name in a circle with the date in Arabic in the surrounding margin; the other has the title, "*The most mighty Sultan,*" on the reverse, and the sultan's name on the obverse (Pl. IX, 8). The calligraphy is of a southern type and this alone distinguishes these coins from Dehlī issues.

[1] Two gold coins are also known of these kings; one is in the British Museum.

IV. COINAGES OF THE DECCAN

The Deccan province, after a series of revolts extending over four years, became finally severed from the Dehlī kingdom in 1347 (A.H. 748). Certain copper coins in the Dehlī style, bearing this date, have been attributed to Nāṣiru-d-dīn Isma'īl, the first officer to assume the state of royalty. But in the same year he was superseded by Sultan 'Alāu-d-dīn Ḥasan Bahmanī, founder of a dynasty which ruled till 1518, when its bloodstained annals as an independent kingdom closed, though nominal sovereigns supported the pretensions of royalty until 1525. The earliest known coin of the dynasty bears the date A.H. 757. The kingdom at the height of its power, under Muḥammad Shāh III (1463-82), extended from the province of Berār in the north to the confines of Mysore in the south, and east to west from sea to sea. Until the time of 'Alāu-d-dīn Aḥmad Shāh II (1435-57) the capital was Kulbarga, renamed by the founder of the kingdom Aḥsanābād; Aḥmad Shāh moved the seat of government to Bīdar, which henceforth, under the name Muḥammadābād, appears on the coinage in place of Aḥsanābād. No other mint names have been found.

The gold and silver coins are fine broad pieces modelled on the tankahs of 'Alāu-d-dīn Muḥammad of Dehlī. In the earlier reigns there is some variety in arrangement and design: the legend on the silver of Aḥmad Shāh I (1422-35), for example, is enclosed in an oval border, and there is a gold piece of the versatile bigot, Fīroz Shāh (1399-1422), corresponding in weight and fabric to Muḥammad bin Tughlaq's heavy issue. But by the reign of Aḥmad Shāh II a single design had been adopted for both metals (Pl. IX, 2); on the obverse are inscribed various titles which changed with each ruler; on the reverse appear the king's name and further titles within a square area; while in the margins are the mint name and date. The legend on the gold coins of Maḥmūd Shāh (1482-1518), perhaps the commonest of the rare Bahmanī gold issues, may serve as an example: obverse, "*Trusting in the Merciful one, the strong, the rich, the mighty Sultan*"; reverse, "*The father of battles, Maḥmūd Shāh, the guardian, the Bahmanī.*" Small silver pieces were struck by the first two rulers, weighing from 15 to 26 grains.

The earliest copper follows closely that of Dehlī, but innovations soon made their appearance, and after the reign of Aḥmad Shāh II coins are found varying from 225 to 27 grains in weight; the copper standard seems to have been continually changed. Some of the titles appearing on the silver are usually to be found on the same ruler's copper, but many varieties in type are found, especially among the issues of Muḥammad I (1358-73) and the later kings; of Maḥmūd Shah seven varieties are known, and seven are also known of Kalīmullah, the last nominal king, struck probably by Amīr Barīd of Bīdar.

During the reign of Maḥmūd Shāh the great kingdom of the Deccan was split up into five separate sultanates. Copper coins of at least three of the Niẓām Shāhs of Aḥmadnagar (1490-1637) are known: they appear to have had mints at Aḥmadnagar, Daulatābād and Burhānābād. The coinage of Gulkanda is confined to a single copper type, struck by the two last Quṭb Shāhī kings, 'Abdullah and Abu-l-Ḥasan; the reverse bears the pathetic legend, "*It has come to an end well and auspiciously.*" The copper coins of the last five 'Ādil Shāhī rulers of Bījāpūr are rather ornate, but usually very ill-struck; small gold pieces bearing a couplet are known of Muḥammad (1627-56). Most interesting of all Bījāpūr coins are the curious silver *Lārīns*,[1] or fish-hook money, issued by 'Alī II, 1656-72 (Pl. IX, 10), which became one of the standard currencies among traders in the Indian Ocean towards the end of the sixteenth century. The coinage of the sultans of the Maldive Islands, whereon they styled themselves "*Sultans of land and sea,*" was based on that of Bījāpūr and survived till the present century.

[1] The name is derived from the port Lār, on the Persian Gulf, where this coin was first struck.

V. THE COINAGE OF THE KINGDOM OF JAUNPŪR

The Eastern (Sharqī) kingdom of Jaunpūr, which also included the modern districts of Gorakhpūr, Tirhut and Bihār, owed its independence to the power and influence of the eunuch, Khwāja-i-Jahān, who was appointed "Lord of the East," by Māḥmūd Shāh II of Dehlī, in 1394. The coinage does not, however, begin till the reign of the third ruler Ibrāhīm (1400-40), and he and his three successors continued to mint till 1476, when Bahlol Lodī overthrew Ḥusain Shāh and re-annexed the province to Dehlī. The bulk of the Jaunpūr coinage consists of billon and copper pieces modelled on those of Dehlī. The commonest billon type has on the obverse the legend, "*The Khalif, the commander of the faithful, may his khalifate be perpetuated*"; the reverse gives the king's name, and on coins of the last three rulers their pedigree as well. Maḥmūd Shāh (1440-58) introduced a type of copper with his name in a circle on the obverse, which was continued by his successors (Pl. IX, 5). Billon coins were struck in the name of Ḥusain Shāh for thirty years after his expulsion from Jaunpūr in 1476 (A.H. 881); and a few copper coins of about the same period bear the name of a rebel, Bārbak Shāh, a brother of Bahlol Lodī. The silver coins of Ibrāhīm and Maḥmūd are extremely scarce. Gold was struck by Ibrāhīm, Maḥmūd and Ḥusain. With the exception of one coin of Ibrāhīm, which follows the ordinary Dehlī model, all three rulers, evidently influenced by their neighbour, Jalālu-d-dīn Muḥammad of Bengal, used the "organ-pipe" arrangement of *tughra* characters for the inscription of the reverse (Pl. IX, 4). The obverse inscription employed by Ibrāhīm and Maḥmūd, "*In the time of the supreme head of Islām, the deputy of the commander of the faithful,*" and the more correct form used by Ḥusain, which omits the words "*the deputy of,*" again show Dehlī influence. Only one coin, a large copper piece of Maḥmūd in the British Museum, is known to bear the mint name Jaunpūr.

VI. THE COINAGE OF MĀLWĀ

Mālwā, annexed to the Dehlī kingdom by 'Alāu-d-din in 1305, became an independent state under the governor, Dilāwar Khān Ghorī, in 1401. His son, Hoshang Shāh (1405-32), initiated the coinage. The province, after incessant wars with Gujarāt, attained its widest limits under the usurping minister, Maḥmūd I, Khiljī (1436-68). But after a civil war, in 1510, a steady decline set in, and in 1530 Bahādur Shāh of Gujarāt captured Mandū, the capital, and the country remained a province of his kingdom for four years. It was next captured by Humāyūn. Then, from 1536 to 1542, it was ruled by a Gujarātī governor, Qādir Shāh. Finally it was governed by Bāz Bahādur, a son of Sher Shāh's nominee, Shujā' Khān, from 1554 to 1560, when it was conquered by Akbar and made a Mughal province.

The first seven Sultans struck coins in all three metals. Maḥmūd I introduced billon, and this was employed also by his three successors. The characteristic feature of the Mālwā coinage is the square shape, also introduced by Maḥmūd I; he and his successor, Ghiyāṣ Shāh (1469-1500), struck both square and round coins, but from the reign of Nāṣir Shāh (1500-10) the square form is used exclusively. The gold pieces of the first two kings follow the Dehlī style. Maḥmūd, however, introduced a new type for the reverse, dividing the face of the coin into two equal parts by lengthening the tail of the last letter "yē" in his name, Khiljī. Ghiyāṣ Shāh used a similar band on both faces (Pl. IX, 3), and this is a mark of almost all succeeding coins in both shapes.

The square base silver pieces of Maḥmūd II (1510-30), with the inscriptions enclosed in circular and octagonal borders, are the finest coins of the series. The rebel, Muhammad II (1515), the Gujarāt king, Bahādur, the governor, Qādir Shāh, and Bāz Bahādur struck copper coins only. The mint name, Shādīābād (Mandū), "City of Delight," is inscribed only on coins of the earlier kings.

With the reign of Ghīyāṣ Shāh a series of ornaments begins to appear on the coinage; the purpose of these is uncertain, but they seem to be connected with the dates of issue. Like the Bahmanīs, the Mālwā sovereigns use elaborate honorific titles for their inscriptions. Perhaps the most striking is one of Maḥmūd I, who calls himself "*The mighty sovereign, the victorious, the exalted in the Faith and in the world, the second Alexander, the right hand of the Khalifate, the defender of the commander of the faithful.*"

The tradition of the square shape lingered on in Mālwā and the neighbourhood long after the extinction of its independence; curious crude little pieces were struck, probably for a century at least, with a mixture of Mughal, Mālwā and Gujarātī inscriptions. Square copper Mughal coins were struck at Ujjain up to the time of Shāh Jahān I, and Saṅgrāma Siṁha of Mewar (1527-32) also modelled his copper coinage on that of Mālwā.

VII. THE COINAGE OF GUJARĀT

Ẓafar Khān, viceroy of the wealthy province of Gujarāt, threw off his allegiance to Sultan Maḥmūd II of Dehlī in 1403, but the first coins known are those of his grandson, Aḥmad I (1411-43), founder of the great city of Aḥmadābād in A.H. 813 and of Aḥmadnagar in A.H. 829. The dynasty reached the culmination of its power in the long reign of Maḥmūd I (1458-1511), who instituted two new mints at Muṣṭafa'ābād in Girnār, and Muḥammadābād (Champānīr). He was succeeded by eight princes, of whom Bahādur Shāh (1526-36) alone showed any ruling ability. The province was added to the Mughal Empire in 1572, but the deposed king, Muẓaffar III, regained his throne for five months eleven years later, and actually struck silver and copper of the Mughal Aḥmadābād type. Coins of nine of the fifteen kings are known.

The coinage, chiefly of silver and copper, at its commencement followed the Dehlī style, but soon developed a characteristic fabric of its own, though the late Dehlī copper type, with the Sultan's name in a square area, never entirely lost its influence in Gujarāt (Pl. IX, 6, 7). The standard seems, however, always to have been a local one, based on the weight of the Gujarātī rati of 1·85 grains. Gold pieces, except those of Maḥmūd III (1553-61; Pl. IX, 6), are rare. Maḥmūd I also employed billon, and his coins are the finest of the series. His silver coins, on which the legends are enclosed in hexagons, scolloped circles and other figures, are very ornate. The inscriptions are for the most part simple; on the obverse appear various titles and formulæ, on the reverse the king's name, sometimes accompanied by his *laqab* (kingly title). The earliest Persian couplet to appear on an Indian coin is found on one of Maḥmūd II, dated A.H. 850. It runs as follows:

So long as the sphere of the seat of the mint, the orb of the sun and moon remains,

May the coin of Maḥmūd Shāh the Sultan, the aid of the Faith, remain.

Perhaps the most interesting of the Gujarāt series are the so-called "pedigree coins," each struck probably for some special occasion, on which the striker traces his descent back to the founder of the dynasty. Only four silver coins of this class have been recorded, two of Aḥmad I, one dated A.H. 828 and the earliest known Gujarāt coin, one of Maḥmūd I, and one of Bahādur Shāh.

Although the majority of coins were probably struck at Aḥmadābād, the name actually occurs only on the copper of Muẓaffar III of the years A.H. 977 and 978 *Aḥmadnagar*, accompanied by an uncertain epithet, is inscribed on the copper of Aḥmad I from A.H. 829 onwards. *Shahr-i-a'ẓam* ("*the very great city*") *Muṣṭafa'ābād* appears on silver and copper, and *Shahr-i-mukarram* (*the illustrious city*) *Muḥammad-ābād* on all the finest silver pieces of Maḥmūd I.

Muẓaffar III granted permission to the Jām of Navānagar to coin "korīs" (*i.e.* copper pieces), provided that they should bear the king's name. Such korīs, bearing debased Gujarāt legends, were also coined for several centuries by the chiefs of Jūnagaḍh and Purbandar.

Fig. 9. Mint marks on Mughal coins.

IX

COINS OF THE SŪRIS AND THE MUGHALS

AFTER the battle of Pānīpat, in 1526, Ẓahīru-d-dīn Bābur's rule in Hindustān, until his death in 1530, was in reality nothing more than a military occupation, and Humāyūn's position during the first ten years of his reign was even more unstable. The silver *shāhrukhīs*, or *dirhams*, of Bābur and Humāyūn, which follow in every respect the Central Asian coinage of the Timurid princes, were obviously struck only as occasion warranted, chiefly at Āgra, Lāhor (Pl. X, 1), Dehlī and Kābul. The interesting camp mint Urdū first appears on a coin of Bābur, an eloquent testimony to the nature of his sovereignty. On the obverse of these coins is the Kalima, enclosed in areas of various shapes with the names of the four orthodox Khalifs or Companions and their attributes[1] in the margins; on the reverse the king's name, also in an area, in the margins various titles, together with the mint and generally the date. Humāyūn's gold are tiny mintless pieces, also of Timurid fabric (Pl. X, 2); a very few of these and some silver dirhams are known of Akbar's first three years. Bābur and Humāyūn's copper coins are anonymous, and were minted chiefly at Āgra, Dehlī, Lāhor and Jaunpūr.

[1] For inscription, cf. Key to Plate X, 1.

Note.—The mint marks in Fig. 9 occur on coins of the following: (1) Humāyūn, Āgra, etc. (2) Shāh 'Ālam II, Shāhjahānābād. (3) Aurangzeb, Multān. (4) East India Company, copied from Mughal coins. (5) Nawābs of Awadh, Muḥammadābād-Banāras. (6) The Kitār—"dagger," Shāh 'Ālam II, Narwar, etc. (7) Aṅkūs—"Elephant-goad"—Marāṭhā coins.

The Afghān Sher Shāh Sūrī, who after the expulsion of Humāyūn in 1540 (A.H. 947), controlled the destinies of Hindustān for five years, was a ruler of great constructive and administrative ability, and the reform of the coinage, though completed by Akbar, was in a great measure due to his genius. His innovations lay chiefly in two directions: first, the introduction of a new standard of 178 grains for silver, and one of about 330 grains for copper, with its half, quarter, eighth and sixteenth parts. These two new coins were subsequently known as the *rupee* and the *dām*. The second innovation was a large increase in the number of the mints: at least twenty-three mint names appear on the Sūrī coins. The object of this extension, probably suggested to Sher Shāh during his residence in Bihār by the Bengal coinage, was no doubt to provide an ocular proof of sovereignty to his subjects in the most distant provinces of his dominions; but the system needed a firm and resolute hand at the centre of government.

Genuine gold coins of the Sūrī kings are exceedingly rare. The rupees are fine broad pieces (Pl. X, 3); the obverse follows the style of Humāyūn's silver; the reverse bears the Sultan's name in a square or circular area, along with the date and the legend, "*May God perpetuate his kingdom*," and below the area the Sultan's name in Hindī, often very faulty.[1] In the margin are inscribed the special titles of the Sultan, and sometimes the mint. On a large number of both silver and copper coins no mint name occurs; some of these seem to be really mintless, the dies of others were too large for the coin discs. On a very common mintless silver type of Islām Shāh (1545-53) and Muḥammad 'Ādil Shāh, the Arabic figures 477 occur in the margin: the significance of these is unknown. A few silver coins of Sher Shāh and Islām Shāh are square; half rupees are extremely scarce; a one-sixteenth piece is also known.

The majority of copper coins bear on the obverse the inscription, "*In the time of the commander of the*

[1] If the area is circular the Hindī inscription appears in the margin.

faithful, the protector of the religion of the Requiter"; on the reverse appear the Sultan's name and titles and the mint (Pl. X, 4). These inscriptions are sometimes contained within square areas.

During the years 1552-56 two nephews and a cousin of Sher Shāh, Muḥammad 'Ādil, Sikandar and Ibrāhīm, contested the throne and struck both copper and silver. Coins of the two last are very rare (Pl. X, 5).

The few coins of Humāyūn's short second reign of six months which have survived show that he had adopted both the new silver and copper standards of the Sūrīs, though he also coined dirhams. With Akbar's accession, in 1556 (A.H. 963), begins the Mughal coinage proper. The special value placed by Muhammadan sovereigns on the privilege of coining has already been noticed; Muḥammad bin Tughlaq used his money as a means of imposing decrees upon his subjects; in a more refined way Akbar used the coinage to propagate his new "Divine" faith; and both he and the cultured Jahāngīr detected in it a ready medium for the expression of their artistic tastes. The importance attached to the currency by the Mughal emperors is further revealed in the full accounts given by Akbar's minister, Abū-l-faẓl, in the *Āīn-i-Akbarī*, and by Jahāngīr in his memoirs, the *Tūzuk-i-Jahāngīrī*, and by the number of references to the subject by historians throughout the whole period. From these and from a study of the coins themselves scholars have collected a mass of materials, from which it is now possible to give a fairly comprehensive account of the Mughal coinage. Abū-l-faẓl and Jahāngīr mention a large number of gold and silver coins, varying from 2,000 tolahs[1] to a few grains in weight. Gigantic pieces are also mentioned by Manucci, Hawkins and others; and Manucci says that they were not current, but that the king (Shāh Jahān) "gave them as presents to the ladies." They were also at times presented to ambassadors, and appear, indeed, to have been merely used as a convenient form in which to store

[1] The tolah in Jahāngīr's time weighed probably between 185 and 187 grains.

treasure. Naturally very few of these pieces have survived, but a silver coin of Aurangzeb is reported to be in Dresden, which weighs five and a half English pounds, and there is a cast of a 200-muhar piece of Shāh Jahān in the British Museum. In the British Museum also are two five-muhar pieces, one of Akbar and one of Jahāngīr, both struck in the Āgra mint. A few double rupees of later emperors, and a ten-rupee piece of Shāh 'Ālam II of Sūrat mint are also known. The standard gold coin of the Mughals was the muhar, of about 170 to 175 grains, the equivalent of nine rupees in Abū-l-faẓl's time. With the exception of a few of Akbar's square issues, which are slightly heavier, and Jahāngīr's experiment during his first five years, when it was raised first by one-fifth to 204 grains, and then by one-fourth to 212·5 grains, the muhar maintains a wonderful consistency of weight and purity to the end of the dynasty. Half and quarter muhars are known of several emperors, and a very few smaller pieces.

The rupee, adopted from Sher Shāh's currency, is the most famous of all Mughal coins. The name occurs only once, on a rupee of Āgra minted in Akbar's forty-seventh year.[1] This, too, maintained its standard of weight, 178 grains, practically unimpaired, although during the reigns of the later emperors some rupees minted by their officers are deficient in purity. The "heavy" rupees of Jahāngīr's early years exceed the normal weight, like the muhars, first by one-fifth and then by one-fourth; and a few slightly heavier than the normal standard were also minted by Shāh 'Ālam Bahādur and Farrukhsiyar in Bihār and Bengal. Halves, quarters, eighths and sixteenths were also struck. In Sūrat the half rupee appears to have been in special demand, and in Akbar's reign the half rupee was also the principal coin issuing from Kābul.

In addition to the regular gold and silver currency, special small pieces were occasionally struck for largesse; the commonest of these is the *niṣār*, struck

[1] Cf. *Lahore Museum Catalogue* (Mughal Emperors), Pl. XXI, iv.

in silver by Jahāngīr, Shāh Jahān, Aurangzeb, Jahāndār and Farrukhsiyar. Gold *niṣārs* are very scarce (Pl. XI, 8). Jahāngīr also issued similar pieces, which he called *Nūr afshān*, "Light scattering," and *Khair qabūl*, "May these alms be accepted" (Pl. X, 12). In 1679 Aurangzeb reimposed the *jizyā*, or poll-tax, on infidels, and, in order to facilitate payment in the orthodox manner, struck the *dirham shar'ī*, "legal dirham," usually square in shape, in a number of mints (Pl. XI, 11). Farrukhsiyar again issued these dirhams, when he re-instituted the poll-tax in the sixth year of his reign. The Mughal copper coinage is based on Sher Shāh's dām of 320 to 330 grains, which, with its half, quarter and eighth, continued to be struck until the fifth year of Aurangzeb, 1663 (A.H. 1073). The name *dām* occurs only once on a half dām of Akbar of Srīnagar mint. The usual term employed is *Fulūs*, "copper money," or *Sikkah fulūs*, "stamped copper money." The names *niṣfī* (half dām), *damrā* (= quarter dām), *damrī* (= one eighth of a dām) also appear on Akbar's copper. Jahāngīr inscribes the word *rawānī* on some of his full and half dāms, and *rā'ij* on his smaller pieces, both meaning simply "current."

Between the forty-fifth and fiftieth years of Akbar's reign were issued, from eight mints, the full *tankah* of 644 grains weight, with its half, quarter, eighth and sixteenth parts, though the large full *tankahs* are known only from Āgra, Dehlī (Pl. X, 10), Aḥmadābād and Bairāt. About the same time Akbar introduced the decimal standard, with his series of four, two and one *tānkī* pieces, struck at Aḥmadābād, Āgra, Kābul and Lāhor; ten *tānkīs* being equal to one full *tankah*.

After the fifth year of Aurangzeb, owing to a rise in the price of copper, the weight of the dām or fulūs was diminished to 220 grains, and this became the accepted standard for southern mints. A few coins of the heavier weight were struck subsequently by Aurangzeb, Shāh 'Ālam Bahādur and Farrukhsiyar. The copper coinage of later emperors until Shāh 'Ālam II's reign is not plentiful.

The early gold and silver coins of Akbar bear the same inscriptions, though there is some variation in their arrangement. Following Bābur's and the Sūrī coinage, the Kalima and Companions' names appear on the obverse, and on the reverse at the beginning of the reign the following inscription, "*Jalālu-d-dīn Muḥammad Akbar, Emperor, champion of the Faith, the mighty Sultan, the illustrious Emperor, may God most High perpetuate the kingdom and the sovereignty.*" Portions of this are dropped later on (Pl. X, 7). Squares, circles, lozenges and other geometrical figures are employed to contain the more important parts of the legend, and the mint name always, and the date generally, appear on the reverse. About the year A.H. 985 the shape of the coins was changed from round to square, but the same inscriptions were retained.

In the year 1579 (A.H. 987) Akbar promulgated his Infallibility Decree, and in the same year appear quarter rupees from the Fatḥpūr, Lāhor, and Aḥmadābād mints, with a new inscription, *Allāhu Akbar*, upon the obverse. From the thirty-second year an expanded form of this, *Allāhu Akbar jalla jalālahu*, "God is great, eminent is His glory," appears on a mintless series of square silver coins (Pl. X, 11); and from the thirty-sixth year it is used regularly on the square issues of the chief mints; later on there is a reversion to the round form. These Ilāhī coins are all dated in Akbar's new regnal era,[1] and also bear the names of the Persian solar months. The custom of issuing coins monthly continues with a few breaks in Jahāngīr's reign until the early years of Shāh Jahān. The round Ilāhī coins, especially those of Āgra, Patna and Lāhor, display considerable artistic merit: certain issues of Āgra of the fiftieth year (Pl. X, 8) are probably the finest of the whole Mughal series. Among the many remarkable coins struck by Akbar may be mentioned the muhar, shaped like a double *Mihrāb*, which appeared from the Āgra mint in A.H. 981 (Pl. X, 6);

[1] This starts from 28th Rab'ī II, A.H. 963, the first year of his reign, but was not instituted until the 29th year. The earliest known coin dated in this era is of the year 31.

the Ilāhī muhar of the fiftieth year, from the same mint, engraved with the figure of a duck (Pl. X, 9); the beautiful "hawk" muhar, struck at Asīrgarh in commemoration of its conquest in the forty-fifth year; and the mintless half-muhar, bearing the figures of Sītā and Rāma. Specimens of all these are in the British Museum. Akbar also initiated the practice of inscribing verse-couplets on the coinage, into which was worked the emperor's name or the mint, or both. These were used by him for only three mints, but with Jahāngīr the practice became general, and forty-seven different couplets of his reign have been recorded (cf. Key to Pl. XI, 2, 3, 4, 5, 6).

Jahāngīr's gold and silver coins in their endless variety are the most ornate of all Mughal coins. Starting with a Kalima obverse, and his name and titles on the reverse (Pl. X, 1), he soon adopted a couplet legend; sometimes the couplet is peculiar to a single mint, sometimes it serves a group of mints. During the fifth and sixth years at Āgra (Pl. XI, 4) and Lāhor the couplets were for a short time changed every month. In the latter year followed a new type, with the emperor's name on the obverse, and the month, date and mint name on the reverse; this remains till the end of the reign on the coins of some mints, but at Āgra, Lāhor, Qandahār and one or two others there is a return to the couplet inscription. For varying periods between the years A.H. 1033 and 1037 the name of the Empress Nūr Jahān is associated in a couplet with that of Jahāngīr on the issues of Āgra, Aḥmadābād, Akbarnagar, Ilahābād, Patna, Sūrat (Pl. XI, 5) and Lāhor.

Jahāngīr seemed to find unceasing zest in novelty: from the sixth to the thirteenth year of his reign the rupees of Āgra were minted in the square and round shape in alternate months. In the thirteenth year appeared the famous Zodiac coins, on which pictorial representations of the signs of the zodiac were substituted for the names of the months on the reverse; this type was retained on the Āgra muhars (Pl. XI, 2) till the seventeenth year. The Zodiac rupees of

Aḥmadābād lasted only for five months during the thirteenth year, while single gold and silver coins of this type are known of Lāhor, Fatḥpūr, Ajmer, Urdū and Kashmīr, of various years up to A.H. 1036. The so-called Bacchanalian and portrait muhars have been recently shown to be insignia presented by Jahāngīr to his courtiers.[1] Some of these are mintless, others were struck at Ajmer. On the obverse of the latter the emperor appears seated cross-legged with a wine-cup in his hand (Pl. XI, 3). The most remarkable of the former, struck in the first year of the reign, bears a full-faced portrait of Akbar on the obverse along with the inscription *Allāhu Akbar*, while a representation of the sun covers the whole of the reverse.[2]

The beauty and rarity of the couplet rupees of Ajmer, Urdū dar rāh-i-Dakan, "The camp on the road to the Deccan" and Mandū, as well as a muhar from the last mint, all struck between the ninth and eleventh years, entitle then to special mention.

Few of Shāh Jahān's coins (A.H. 1037-1068) are of any artistic merit. The earliest form of his gold and silver has the Kalima and mint name on the obverse, and the emperor's name and titles on the reverse (Pl. XI, 7). From the second to the fifth year solar months[3] were inscribed. From the fifth year to the end of the reign, except at the Tatta mint, where the earlier style was retained, Shāh Jahān employed a type, endless in its varieties, in which squares, circles, lozenges form borders enclosing the Kalima on the obverse and the king's name on the reverse, while the names of the companions and their epithets are restored and appear in the obverse margins. The square border form of this type was also employed by Aurangzeb's rivals, Murād Bakhsh and Shāh Shujā' (Pl. XI, 10); and Aurangzeb uses square areas to contain the

[1] By S. H. Hodivala, *Historical Studies in Mughal Numismatics*, Memoir No. II, Numismatic Society of India, Calcutta, 1923.

[2] In the possession of Mr. H. Nelson Wright, I.C.S.

[3] Jahāngīr used a solar era of his own, starting from the date of his accession. The years on Shāh Jahān's coins are lunar. Cf. Hodivala, *loc-cit.*

inscriptions on his earlier rupees of Akbarābād (Āgra) and Jūnagarh, and for a few coins of three other mints.

The coins of Aurangzeb (A.H. 1068-1119) and his successors are, with a very few exceptions, monotonous in the extreme. On the obverse there is either a couplet containing the king's name, or this inscription: "*The blessed coin of . . . ,*" followed by the name of the particular king. On the reverse appears, with very occasional variations, the following: "*Struck at* (the mint name), *in the year* (the regnal year) *of the accession associated with prosperity.*" The Hijrī date is placed on the obverse (Pl. XI, 9). Pretentious personal titles are of infrequent occurrence on Mughal coins. Nevertheless the pretenders, Murād Bakhsh and Shāh Shujā‘, style themselves "The Second Alexander." Shāh Jahān I, in imitation of his ancestor Tīmūr, who adopted the title "*Lord of the fortunate conjunction*" (*i.e.* of the planets), called himself "*The Second Lord of the fortunate conjunction*" (*Ṣāḥib-i-qirān ṣānī*), and eight later emperors followed his example. Jahāngīr used his princely name, Salīm, on his earliest coins from the Aḥmadābād mint (Pl. XI, 6) and on a half rupee of Kābul. On a unique rupee of Lāhor of Shāh Jahān I's first year occurs the name Khurram, while Shāh ‘Ālam Bahādur placed his pre-regnal name, Mu‘aẓẓam, on coins of his first year of Tatta and Murshidābād.

Coins of special interest and rarity are those struck by pretenders, particularly the rupees of Dāwar Bakhsh of Lāhor, A.H. 1037; the coins of Shāh Shujā‘, 1068, of Bīdār Bakht, 1202-1203; and the rupee of Jahāngīrnagar, struck by ‘Aẓīmu-sh-shān in 1124. Commemorative coins of the later emperors are exceedingly scarce, but the entry of Lord Lake into Dehlī, in 1803, was marked on Shāh ‘Ālam II's gold and silver coinage of the forty-seventh year by enclosing the obverse and reverse inscriptions within a wreath of roses, shamrocks and thistles (Pl. XII, 1).

The fabric of the copper coins is, in general, rude. With the exception of the *tankah* and *tānkī* issues, Akbar's copper is anonymous; his Ilāhī copper, like the silver and gold, was dated in the new era and issued monthly. Some of Jahāngīr's *rawānīs*, especially those from the Ajmer mint, have pretensions to artistic merit. His copper issues, and those of succeeding kings, with the exception of a few of Aurangzeb's, have the king's name and Hijrī date on the obverse, and the mint and regnal year on the reverse.

The Hijrī era was used by all emperors and usually the regnal year is inscribed as well. For his later coins, as has been seen, Akbar employed his own Divine era, Jahāngīr and Shāh Jahān I each used similar eras, but as they place the Hijrī year along with the solar months on the coins the calculation of the dates is somewhat confusing.

From the time of Humāyūn onwards there appear on the coinage certain marks, sometimes called mint-marks, but perhaps more properly designated ornaments (Fig. 9). The purpose of these on the earlier issues is uncertain, later on they sometimes marked a change of mint-masters; others appear to have been really distinctive mint marks, such as that which appears on Shāh 'Ālam II's Shāhjahānābād coins (Fig. 9, 2).

Perhaps the most distinctive feature of the Mughal coinage is the diversity of mints. Akbar's known mints number seventy-six. Copper was struck in fifty-nine of these, the largest number recorded for any emperor, while silver is known from thirty-nine. Aurangzeb's conquests in the Deccan raised the silver mints to seventy, whereas copper mints sank to twenty-four. For the remaining emperors mints for silver average about fifty until Shāh 'Ālam II's time, when they rose to eighty; most of these, however, were not under the imperial control. The puppet emperors, Akbar II and Bahādur Shāh, were permitted by the East India Company to strike coins only in their prison capital, Shāhjahānābād (Dehlī). Altogether over two hundred mints are known, but the greater number of these were worked only occasionally; Āgra, Dehlī, Lāhor and Aḥmadābād alone struck coin continuously throughout the Mughal period. To these may be added Sūrat, Ilahābād, Jahāngīrnagar and Akbarnagar from Jahāngīr's reign,

Multān from the reign of Shāh Jahān I, and Itāwah and Barelī from the time of Aurangzeb. The practice of giving mint towns honorific titles, in vogue with the early Muhammadan Sultans, was continued by the Mughals. Thus Dehlī became, on being selected as the capital of the empire by Shāh Jahān I, in A.H. 1048, Shāhjahānābād. In the second year of the same reign Āgra became Akbarābād. Epithets were also frequently attached to mint names. *Dāru-l-khilāfat*, "Seat of the Khalifate," *i.e.* "Chief City," is applied to twelve mints besides Āgra. *Dāru-s-saltanat* is the usual epithet of Lāhor. After A.H. 1100 Aurangzeb changed the name of Aurangābād to Khujista Bunyād, "The fortunate foundation," the only example of a Mughal mint called solely by an honorific epithet.

The great system of coinage illustrated by the Mughals, operating over such wide territories, needed, as has been already remarked, a master hand to control it. With the dissensions which set in between rival claimants to the empire on the death of Aurangzeb, the controlling power was weakened. The diminished resources of his treasury compelled the emperor, Farrukhsiyar (1713-19), to adopt the fatal policy of farming out the mints. This gave the *coup de grâce* to the system, and henceforward, as will be related in the next chapter, we find independent, and semi-independent chiefs and states striking coins of their own, but always with the nominal consent of the Dehlī emperor, and almost invariably in his name. Not until the nineteenth century was the Mughal style and superscription generally discarded.

Such was the coinage of the "Great Mogul." Considering it as the output of a single dynasty, which maintained the high standard and purity of its gold and silver for three hundred years, considering also its variety, the number of its mints, the artistic merit of some of its series, the influence it exerted on contemporary and subsequent coinages, and the importance of its standard coin—the rupee—in the commerce of to-day, the Mughal currency surely deserves to rank as one of the great coinages of the world.

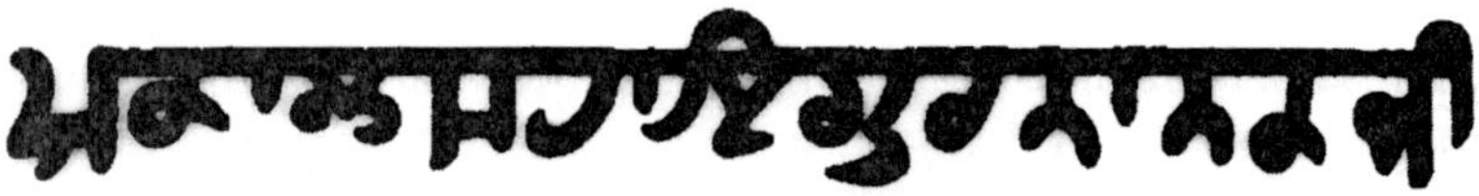

Fig. 10. Gurmukhī Script on Sikh Coins, *Akāl Sahāī : Gūrū Nānakjī*.

X

CONTEMPORARIES AND SUCCESSORS OF THE MUGHALS

THE neighbours of the Mughals were not slow to recognise the excellence of their coinage. Even the Ṣafavī monarchs of Persia adopted certain features. The East Himalayan kingdom of Assam, hitherto content to use the money of Bengal, and the adjacent state of Nepāl, which had been without a coinage of its own for centuries, within fifty years of Akbar's accession had both adopted the rupee standard.

I. THE COINAGE OF ASSAM

Assam, the ancient Kāmarūpa, had been invaded in A.D. 1228 by the Ahoms, a Shan tribe from Burma, and finally subdued by them in 1540. By the year 1695 the royal family had definitely submitted to the influence of Hinduism. Previously to that date, expression of devotion to the tribal gods Lengdun, Tara and Phatuceng appears on the coins; but the reverse legend of a coin of the Śaka year 1618 (A.D. 1696), struck by Rudra Siṁha (1696-1714), runs as follows, in the highly poetical Sanskrit so characteristic of later coin inscriptions: "*A bee on the nectar of the feet of Hara and Gaurī.*"

The earliest known coins are those of Śuklenmung (1539-52), but these and the money of his five successors were struck for ceremonial occasions, probably only at the coronation, and a yearly coinage was first introduced by Rudra Siṁha. The strange octagonal shape of the coins is said to owe its origin to a statement in the Yoginī Tantra, which describes the Ahom country as octagonal. Some of the smaller coins are, however, round, and Śiva Siṁha, for a coin of Ś. 1651, on which he associates the name of his queen, Pramatheśvarī, and Rājeśvara Siṁha (1751-69), for two of his issues, adopted the square Mughal form and style with legends in Persian. The inscription on Śiva Siṁha's coin is as follows: obverse, *Shāh Sheo Singh struck coin like the sun by order of the Queen Pramatheśvarī Shāh*; reverse, *In the year 15 of the fortunate reign at Gargāon 1651* (= A.D. 1729). For this the Nūr Jahān issues of Jahāngīr were obviously the model. With the exception of a coin of Śuklenmung, all gold and silver was struck to a standard of 176 grains, and half, quarter, eighth, and even smaller fractional pieces were minted. Several of the earlier Rājas employed the Ahom language and script for their legends. Sanskrit written in the Bengālī script was first used by Sūrya Nārāyaṇa (1611-49). Pramatta Siṁha (1744-51) and Rājeśvara Siṁha employ both, but after the coronation ceremony of the latter Sanskrit alone was used. The legends, in either script, are always enclosed within dotted borders (Pl. XII, 8). These thick rather solid-looking coins, though attractive on account of their unusual shape, are entirely without artistic merit; they ceased to be minted with the cession of Assam to the British in 1826. The broad round silver pieces of the Rājas of Jaintia (Jayantāpura) of the eighteenth century, and the coins of the hill state of Tipperah, bear legends similar in style to the Assamese Sanskrit coins, and, like them, are dated in the Śaka era. The dates on the Ahom coins of Assam are reckoned according to the Jovian cycle of sixty years.

II. THE COINAGE OF NEPĀL

The considerable Mughal influence exhibited in the modern coinage of the Malla kings of Nepāl, which starts in the early years of the seventeenth century, finds expression in the native legend which affirms that

Rāja Mahendra Malla of Kāthmāṇḍū obtained permission to strike coins from the Dehlī court. Although none of his money has come to light, the story gains some support from the weight of the early Nepalese coins, which are all half-rupees, and from a curious piece of Pratāpa Malla of Kāthmāṇḍū (1639-89), which imitates Jahāngīr's coinage, even adopting fragments of the Persian inscription.

Nepāl, at the period when the coinage begins, was divided into three principalities—Bhatgāon, Pātan and Kāthmāṇḍū—and probably the earliest coins are those of Lakshmī Narasiṁha, ruler of the last province (1595-1639), although the earliest date, Nepālī Samvat[1] 751 (= A.D. 1631) appears on one struck by Siddhi Narasiṁha of Pātan. The usual design on the coins, perhaps suggested by some of Akbar's and Jahāngīr's issues, consists of elaborate geometrically ornamented borders surrounding a central square or circle, with the legends in Nāgarī fitted into the spaces left in the design. On the obverse appear the king's name, titles and date, and on the reverse various symbols, accompanied sometimes by a further title or a religious formula. The Gūrkhas, who conquered the country in 1768, continued the style of their predecessors (Pl. XII, 6), but occasionally struck full as well as the ordinary half-rupees. Gīrvāṇ Yuddha Vikrama (1799-1816) and Surendra Vikrama (1847-81) also struck gold similar in design to the silver coins, and the latter introduced a copper currency.

The silver *tang-ka* (tankah) of Tibet was directly imitated from the coinage of Jagajjaya Malla of Kāthmāṇḍū (1702-32).

III. SUCCESSORS TO THE MUGHALS

The confusion into which the coinage of India fell on the break up of the Mughal power, when independent mints sprang up in every part of their wide dominions, may be gathered from the calculation made

[1] This Nepālī or Newār era was introduced by Rāja Rāghavadeva in A.D. 879.

in the early part of the nineteenth century, that there were no less than 994 different gold and silver coins, old and new, passing as current in the country. The complexity of the subject is further accentuated by the impossibility of distinguishing at present the earlier coins of independent mints from the imperial issues. Later on, the gradual debasement, caused by the addition of special local marks and the evolution of distinctive types in certain states, makes classification easier. Few of these coinages have hitherto been treated comprehensively, and all that can be attempted here is a bare outline, according more detailed treatment only to the more considerable moneying states.

The papers of the East India Company, fortunately, have preserved for us a record of events typical of what was taking place in many parts of India. They show that, besides coining the South Indian pagodas, already noticed, and copper and silver coins in European style, the English factories were early engaged in reproducing the rupees of the Mughal emperors. The first which can be fixed with any certainty are those from the mint of Bombay, or Mumbai, as it appears on the coins, opened in the reign of Farrukhsiyar (1713-19); and in 1742 the emperor, Muḥammad Shāh, granted the Company a *sanad* permitting them to coin Arkāt rupees. Gradually the Company assumed control of all mints within its increasing territories. In 1765, for example, after the battle of Buxar it took over the Bengal mints. Uniformity of standard was maintained, first by engraving special marks on the coins (Fig. 9, 4), and then by fixing the regnal year.[1] Thus the gold and silver coins of the Banāras mint of the Hijrī years 1190 to 1229 all bear the same regnal date 17.[2] So also the year 19

[1] This was to stop peculation on the part of money-changers, bankers and even revenue collectors, who made a rebate on all rupees not of the current year.

[2] On the Banāras coins the actual regnal date, *i.e.* of Shāh 'Ālam II, is added beneath the conventional date 17; this was not adopted for other mints.

was fixed for the Murshidābād mint, the year 45 for Farrukhābād. These coins, still inscribed with the Mughal emperor's name, became more and more European in style (Pl. XII, 9), those of Farrukhābād being even struck with a milled edge, until finally superseded by the British Imperial currency of 1835.

A similar evolution, but in the direction of deterioration, can be traced in the issues of the Marāṭhās, Rājpūts, and other powers. The Marāṭhās seized the important mint of Aḥmadābād in 1752; and the coins struck there in the Mughal style (until it was closed by the British in 1835) all bear as a characteristic mark the "Ankūs," or elephant-goad. The Peshwa also had a mint at Pūna; and numerous private mints in Mahārāsṭhra, some striking pagodas and fanams as well as rupees, were worked with or without his permission. Other Marāṭhā mints were those of the Bhonsla Rājas at Katak in Orissa and at Nāgpūr; rupees of the latter bear the mint-name Sūrat. So also the Gaikwār had a mint at Baroda, Scindia at Ujjain and later on at Gwāliār, Holkār at Indor. Jaśwant Rāo Holkār issued, in 1806, a notable rupee with Sanskrit legends on both obverse and reverse (Pl. XII, 7).

Numerous Rājpūt states copied the imperial coinage in their local mints, Jaipūr (opened about 1742), Bīkāner, Jodhpūr, and many others; but in the nineteenth century the names of the ruling chiefs were substituted for that of the titular emperor. Silver and gold were struck in the emperor's name by the Niẓāms of Ḥaidarābād, who were content to distinguish their several issues by the addition of their initials (Pl. XII, 4) until 1857, after which the full name of the Niẓām took the place of the emperor's. The Rohillas during the period of their ascendancy had a group of mints in Rohilkhand, the chief of which were Najībābād, Murādābād, Barelī and Sahāranpūr. The copper coinage of these independent states is excessively crude, and the practice of striking to local standards, which began under the later Mughals, now became general. The copper mints were probably entirely in private hands,

Here it will be convenient to deal with a coinage, which, though partially of Mughal lineage in other respects, stands by itself. The reign of Tīpū Sulṭān of Mysore, though lasting only sixteen years (1782-99), was productive of one of the most remarkable individual coinages in the history of India, comparable in many ways to that of Muḥammad bin Tughlaq. His father, Ḥaidar 'Alī, as we have already seen (Chap. VI), struck pagodas and fanams. Tīpū continued to strike both these, retaining the initial "hē" of Ḥaidar's name, but adding a mint name on the obverse or reverse (Pl. VI, 10). In addition, he coined muhars and half muhars, in silver the double and full rupee, with its half, quarter, eighth, sixteenth and thirty-second parts, and in copper pieces of 40, 20,[1] 10, 5 and 2½ cash. The 40-cash piece weighed 340 grains. To each of these coins, following perhaps the example of Jahāngīr, he gave a special name. The pagoda, equal to the quarter of a muhar, he called, for instance, *Fārūqī*; the double rupee, *Ḥaidarī*; the rupee, *Aḥmadī*; the 20-cash piece, *Zohra*; and so on. The Persian inscriptions on gold and silver are religious in character, that on the rupee runs as follows: obverse, *The religion of Aḥmad* (*i.e. Islām*) *is illumined in the world by the victory of Ḥaidar, struck at Nagar, the cyclic year Dalv, the Hijrī year 1200*; reverse, *He is the Sultan, the unique, the just; the third of Bahārī, the year Dalv, the regnal year 4*. For his copper coins Tīpū adopted the elephant device of the Wodeyar kings of Mysore (1578-1733), and the animal appears in various attitudes on the obverse, sometimes to right, sometimes to left, with trunk raised, and with trunk lowered. On the 40-cash pieces he carries a flag. The reverse gives the mint and, later in the reign, the distinctive name of the coin also (Pl. XII, 5).

At least thirteen mints were working under Tīpū, the most important being Pattan (Seringapatam), Nagar (Bednūr), and Bangalūr; for some mints merely

[1] The 20-cash piece had been struck by Ḥaidar 'Alī in the last two years of his reign, A.H. 1195-96. Cf. J. R. Henderson, *The Coins of Ḥaidar 'Alī and Tīpū Sulṭān*, Madras, 1921, p. 5.

honorific titles appear, thus *Naẓarbār*, "scattering favour," for Mysore.

The most remarkable and perplexing of Tīpū's innovations was his method of dating the coins. For this purpose he used the Jovian cycle of sixty years, according to the Telugū reckoning, inventing special names for each of the sixteen years of his reign, in accordance with their correspondence with that cycle, and composing the names at different periods from the letters supplied by the two systems of numeration known as *abjad* and *abtaṣ*. For the first four years of his reign, when he employed the *abjad* system, he also dated his coins in the Hijrī era; in the fifth year he invented a new era, the Maulūdī, reckoned from the date of Muḥammad's birth in A.D. 571; dates in this era appear written from right to left. The execution of most of Tīpū's coins is exceptionally good.

Kṛishṇa Rāja Udayar (1799-1868), the restored Rāja of Mysore, for a time continued the elephant copper pieces of Tīpū, but later changed the device for a lion. Kanarese inscriptions (Fig. 6) were, however, at once substituted for Persian.

We must now turn to Hindustān proper. Both Nādir Shāh, in 1739, and Aḥmad Shāh Durrānī (1748-67) and his successors struck rupees and muhars to the Mug͟hal standard for the districts they temporarily occupied. Nādir's issues are Persian in fabric, but the Durrānī coins, struck at Shāhjahānābād (Pl. XII, 2), Farruk͟hābād, Lāhor, Multān, Kābul, and several other mints, are largely Mug͟hal in style. On the whole, the issues of these princes, especially those of Qandahār and Peshāwar and the rare pieces of the pretenders, Sulaimān and Humāyūn, reach a much higher artistic level than the contemporary Mug͟hal coins.

One of the most important results of Aḥmad Shāh's repeated invasions of the Panjāb was the formation of the Sikh League, known as the K͟hālsā. After the seventh invasion, in 1764, the League assumed the right of coinage; and from that date till 1777, with a gap of two years, 1766-67, for Aḥmad Shāh's last invasion, "Gobindshāhī" rupees were struck at Lāhor, so called from the name of the Gūrū Gobind being included in the Persian couplet, which formed the inscription. Amritsar, *Ambratsar* on the coins, became a mint in 1777. Its earliest rupees, known as "Nānakshāhī," bore a different couplet (Pl. XII, 10). A few coins were also struck at Anandgarh. All Sikh coins are dated in the Samvat era.[1] The coins of Rañjīt Siṅgh (1799-1839) are of two distinct kinds, those with Persian (often very faulty) and those with Gurmukhī[2] inscriptions. Rupees of the Persian couplet type appear regularly from the mints of Lāhor and Amritsar throughout his reign, from Multān after 1818, from Kashmīr after 1819; and a few rupees are known from Peshāwar, Jhaṅg and Pind Dādan Khān. The king's name was never inscribed on the coinage; but the characteristic Sikh "leaf" mark makes its appearance upon his earliest rupee, dated S. 1857 (=A.D. 1800). During the Samvat years 1861-63, first a peacock's tail and then a thumb-mirror appears on the Amritsar rupees; these are said to bear reference to Rañjīt's favourite dancing-girl, Mora. A curious rupee of Lāhor of S. 1885 displays the figures of Gūrū Nānak and his Muhammadan follower, Mardānā. Rañjīt Siṅgh also coined muhars similar in style to the rupees.

About the year S. 1885, apparently, the Gurmukhī coins were introduced. A few gold and silver coins are known, but most are copper, some weighing as much as 600 grains. The inscriptions are generally religious in character; the commonest is *Akāl Sahāī, Gūrū Nānakjī*, "O, Eternal one help us! Guru Nānakjī!"[3] The reverse gives the date and mint, generally Ambratsar. The script is usually very crude, and the "leaf" mark is almost invariably present. Some coins, like those of Kashmīr, have bilingual legends in Persian

[1] The Samvat, which corresponds with the Vikrama era, begins in 58 B.C.

[2] Gurmukhī is a Panjāb provincial form of the Nāgarī script (cf. Fig. 10).

[3] The two parts of this legend are quite separate in sense.

and Gurmukhī. Rupees of the Persian couplet type continued to be struck after Rañjīt's death, in S. 1896, till S. 1905 (= A.D. 1848). The chiefs of the Sikh states, Patiāla, Jhind, Nābha and Kaital, and the Dogra Rājas of Kashmīr, after A.D. 1846, also coined rupees of this type. On some of these last was inscribed, on account of its supposed talismanic power, the Christian monogram I.H.S.

In conclusion, we must consider the coins of the Nawāb-wazīrs and kings of Oudh or Awadh. The existence of this province as a separate principality began in 1720, when the wazīr, S'ādat Khān, was created Ṣūbahdār. From 1754 to 1775 the Mughal mint of Muḥammadābād-Banāras was under the control of the third Nawāb-wazīr Shujā'u-d-daula. From 1784 till 1818 succeeding nawābs continued to mint in Lakhnau (Lucknow) the famous "Machhlīdār" rupees, so called from the fish (Fig. 9, 5), the royal badge of Awadh, appearing on the reverse. All of these bear the regnal date 26, and continue the mint name Banāras. Other mints worked by the nawābs from time to time were Barelī, after 1784, Ilahābād, 1776-1780, and Āṣafnagar.

In 1818 Lord Hastings persuaded Ghāzīu-d-dīn Ḥaidar to assume the title of king, and from that time the regal series of coins begins. The royal arms of Awadh, in various forms, appear on the obverse of gold, silver and copper of Ghāzīu-d-dīn and his four successors, until the forced abdication of the last king, Wājid 'Alī Shāh, in 1856. On the reverse, the inscription, following the Mughal example, takes the form of a couplet; and silver and gold are struck to the Mughal standard (Pl. XII, 3). Fractional pieces of the rupee and muhar were struck in all reigns. Though better executed and finer in metal than those of most other successors of the Mughals, these coins display a certain monotony, all denominations in the three metals following the prescribed pattern for the reign. Certain modifications in the inscription, however, take place from time to time. The coins of Wājid 'Alī Shāh's seventh and eighth years, of which five denominations in each metal are known, are probably the finest of the series.

Two large silver medals are associated with the Awadh dynasty, the first commemorating Shujā'u-d-daula's victory over the Rohillas at Mirān Katra, in 1774, the second struck by Ghāzīu-d-dīn Ḥaidar, in honour of his coronation on 1st Muḥarram A.H. 1235. On the obverse of the latter is an ornate and very realistic portrait of the king, and on the reverse the arms of Awadh. Certain "Machhlīdār" rupees and muhars, bearing the date A.H. 1229, on which the mint name *Ṣūbah Awadh* occurs, are believed to have been minted by the Lucknow mutineers. It is not unfitting that this short history of Indian coins should close with a description of the money of the Awadh kings; for this latest scion of the great Mughal currency not only received its sanction from an English Governor-General, but manifested, in the adoption of armorial bearings of a Western type for its obverse, the beginning of that European influence, which, later on in the nineteenth century, was to revolutionise the coin types of the few Indian states, Ḥaidarābād, Travancore, Gwāliār, Alwar, Baroda, etc., which retained the right of minting after the introduction of the British Imperial currency.

SELECT BIBLIOGRAPHY

GENERAL

J. PRINSEP : *Essays in Indian Aniquities*, Ed. E. THOMAS, London, 1858 ; E. J. RAPSON : *Indian Coins* (*Grundriss der Indo-Arischen Philologie und Altertumskunde*), Strassburg, 1897 ; C. J. RODGERS : *Coin Collecting in Northern India*, Allahabad, 1894 ; V. A. SMITH : *Catalogue of the Coins in the Indian Museum*, Calcutta, Vol. I, Oxford, 1906 (for Chaps. I—VI and X); E. THOMAS: "Ancient Indian Weights" (= *International Numismata Orientalia*, I, Part i), 1865.

SPECIAL

CHAP. I.—A. CUNNINGHAM : Coins of Ancient India, 1891; E. J. RAPSON : *Catalogue of the Coins of the Andhra Dynasty, the Western Kṣatrapas, etc., in the British Museum*, London, 1908 ; W. THEOBALD : "Notes on Some of the Symbols found on the Punch-marked Coins of Hindustan," *J.A.S B.*, 1890, p. 181 ; E. H. WALSH : "An Examination of a Find of Punch-marked Coins in Patna City," *Journal of the Bihar and Orissa Research Society*, 1919, p. 16, p. 463.

CHAPS. II-III.—A. CUNNINGHAM : "Coins of Alexander's Successors in the East," 1873 (= *Num. Chron.*, 1868-1873) ; id. : "Coins of the Indo-Scythians," 1892 (= *Num Chron.*, 1888-1892); P. GARDNER : *Catalogue of Indian Coins in the British Museum : Greek and Scythic Kings of Bactria and India*, London, 1886 ; E. J. RAPSON : *Cambridge History of India*, Vol. I, Chaps. XXII, XXIII ; R. B. WHITEHEAD : *Catalogue of Coins in the Panjāb Museum, Lahore*, Vol. I, Oxford, 1914.

CHAP. IV.—J. ALLAN : *Catalogue of the Coins of the Gupta Dynasties in the British Museum*, London, 1914.

CHAP. V.—R. BURN: "Some Coins of the Maukharīs and of the Thanesar Line," *J.R.A.S.*, 1906, p. 843 ; A. CUNNINGHAM: "Coins of the Later Indo-Scythians," 1894 (= *Num. Chron.*, 1893-1894) ; id.: "Coins of Mediæval India," 1894 ; C. J. RODGERS : "Coins of the Mahārājahs of Kashmir," *J.A.S.B.*, 1897, p. 277 ; id.: "Coins of the Mahārājahs of Kāngra," *J.A.S.B.*, 1880, p. 10.

CHAP. VI.—G. BIDIE: "The Pagoda or Varāha Coins of Southern India," *J.A.S.B.*, 1883, p. 33 ; W. ELLIOT : "Coins of Southern India," 1886 (= *International Numismata Orientalia*

III, Part 2); E. HULTZCH: "The Coins of the Kings of Vijayanagar," *I.A.*, 1891, p. 301; id.: "South Indian Copper Coins," *I.A.*, 1892, p. 321; id.: "Miscellaneous South Indian Coins," *I.A.*, 1896, p. 317; R. P. JACKSON: "The Dominions, Emblems and Coins of the South Indian Dynasties," 1913 (= *British Numismatic Journal*, 1913); E. LOVENTHAL: *The Coins of Tinnevelly*, Madras, 1888; T. W. RHYS-DAVIDS: "Ancient Coins and Measures of Ceylon," 1877 (= *International Numismatia Orientalia*, I, Part 6); R. H. C. TUFNELL: *Hints to Coin Collectors in Southern India*, Madras, 1889.

CHAP. VII.—S. LANE POOLE: *Catalogue of Coins in the British Museum, Sultans of Dehli*, London, 1884; E. THOMAS: *Chronicles of the Pathan Kings of Dehli*, London, 1871; C. J. RODGERS: "Coins Supplementary to Thomas, Chronicles of the Pathan Kings," Nos. I—VI., *J.A.S.B.*, 1880-1896; H. N. WRIGHT: *Catalogue of the Coins in the Indian Museum, Calcutta*, Vol. II, Oxford, 1907; id.: "Addenda to the Series of Coins of the Pathān Sultāns of Dehlī," *J.R.A.S.*, p. 481, p. 769.

CHAP. VIII.—S. LANE POOLE: *Catalogue of Coins of the Muhammudan States of India in the British Museum*, London, 1885; H. N. WRIGHT: *Catalogue of the Coins in the Indian Museum, Calcutta*, Vol. II, Oxford, 1907. **Bengal.**—E. THOMAS: "The Initial Coinage of Bengal," *J.A.S.B.*, 1867, p. 1, 1873, p. 343; A. F. R. HOERNLE: "A New Find of Muhammadan Coins of Bengal" (2 papers), *J.A.S.B.*, 1881, p. 53, 1883, p. 211. **Kashmir.**—C. J. RODGERS: "The Square Coins of the Muhammadan Kings of Kashmir," *J.A.S.B.*, 1885, p. 92. **Bahmanis.**—O. CODRINGTON: "Coins of the Bahmani Dynasty," *Num. Chron.*, 1898, p. 259; J. GIBBS: "Gold and Silver Coins of the Bahmanī Dynasty," *Num. Chron.*, 1881. **Gujarat.**—G. P. TAYLOR: "Coins of the Gujarāt Saltanat," *J.B.B.R.A.S.*, 1904, p. 278. **Malwa.**—L. WHITE KING: "History and Coinage of Mālwā," *Num. Chron.*, 1903, p. 356, 1904, p. 62. **Ma'bar.**—E. HULTZCH: "Coinage of the Sultans of Madura," *J.R.A.S.*, 1909, p. 667.

CHAP. IX.—C. J. BROWN: *Catalogue of the Mughal Coins in the Provincial Museum, Lucknow*, 2 Vols., Oxford, 1920; S. LANE POOLE: *Catalogue of the Coins of the Moghul Emperors in the British Museum*, London, 1892; R. B. WHITEHEAD: *Catalogue of the Coins of the Mughal Emperors in the Panjāb Museum, Lahore*, Oxford, 1914; id.: "The Mint Towns of the Mughal Emperors of India," *J.A.S.B.*, 1912, p. 425; H. N. WRIGHT: *Catalogue of the Coins in the Indian Museum, Calcutta*, Vol. III, Oxford, 1908. [Also a large number of articles scattered through the *J.R.A.S.*, *I.A.*, *J.A.S.B.*, especially the Numismatic Supplements to the last, starting from 1904.]

CHAP. X.—J. ALLAN: "The Coinage of Assam," *Num. Chron.*, 1909, p. 300; C. J. BROWN: "The Coins of the Kings of Awadh," *Num. Supp.*, XVIII, *J.A.S.B.*, 1912; M. LONGWORTH

DAMES: "Coins of the Durrānīs," *Num. Chron.*, Vol. VIII, 3rd series, p. 325; C. J. RODGERS: "On the Coins of the Sikhs," *J.A.S.B.*, 1881, p. 71. **East India Company.**—E. THURSTON: "History of the East India Company Coinage," *J.A.S.B.*, 1893, p. 52; id.: *History of the Coinage of the Territories of the E.I.C. in the Indian Peninsula and Catalogue of the Coins in the Madras Museum*, Madras, 1890. **Marathas.**—A. MASTER: "The Post-Mughal Coins of Aḥmadābād, *Num. Supp.*, XXII, *J.A.S.B.*, 1914; M. G. RANADE: "Currencies and Mints Under Mahratta Rule, *J.B.B.R.A.S.*, 1902, p. 191; G. P. TAYLOR: "On the Baroda Coins of the Last Six Gaikwars," *Num. Supp.*, XVIII, *J.A.S.B.*, 1912. **Rajputana.**—A. F. R. HOERNLE: "Notes on Coins of Native States, *J.A.S.B.*, 1897, p 261; W. W. WEBB: *The Currencies of the Hindu States of Rajputana*, London, 1893. **Tipu Sultan.**—R. P. JACKSON: "Coin Collecting in Mysore," *British Numismatic Journal*, 1909; G. P. TAYLOR: "The Coins of Tīpū Sulṭān" (*Occasional Memoirs of the Numismatic Society of India*), 1914.

CHAP. VII-X.—W. H. VALENTINE: *The Copper Coins of India*, I, II, London, 1914.

PRINCIPAL COLLECTIONS OF INDIAN COINS

India.—Indian Museum, Calcutta (all classes); Dehli Museum of Archæology (Sultans of Dehlī, Mughals); Panjāb Museum, Lahore (Indo-Greeks, Śakas, Pahlavas, Sultans of Dehlī, Mughals, Sikhs); Provincial Museum, Lucknow (Ancient Indian, Guptas, Sultans of Dehlī, Mughals, Awadh); Government Central Museum, Madras (South Indian, Ceylon, Mysore, East India Company, Mughals, Sultans of Dehlī, Indo-Portuguese); Prince of Wales' Museum, Bombay (Gujarāt, Mughals, Marāṭhas); Provincial Museum, Shillong (Sultans of Bengal, Assam, Koch, Jaintia); Central Museum, Nagpur (Sultans of Dehlī, Mughals, Marāṭhas, Bahmanīs); Dacca Museum (Sultans of Bengal); Patna Museum (Punch-marked series, Mughals, Sultans of Dehlī, Bengal Sultans); Peshawar Museum (Indo-Greeks, Śakas, Pahlavas, Mughals, Durrānīs), Macmahon Museum, Quetta (Durrānīs, Mughals, Bārakzāīs).

London.—British Museum (all classes).

Continent.—Bibliotheque Nationale, Paris; Kaiser Friedrich Museum, Berlin.

America.—American Numismatic Society's Collection, New York.

INDEX

PRINTED AT THE WESLEYAN MISSION PRESS, MYSORE CITY.

KEY TO PLATE I

1. Round punch-marked coin. AR. Wt. about 50 grs.

   Obv., an animal, solar symbol, etc.

   Rev., three symbols.

2. Rectangular punch-marked coin. AR.

   Obv., bull, solar symbol, etc.

   Rev., several indistinct symbols.

3. Pair of cast coins, showing join. Æ.

   Obv., three-arched chaitya, crescent above.

   Rev., elephant to left.

4. Pañchāla: Phalgunimitra. Æ. Wt. about 220 grs.

   Obv., figure standing on lotus, to left a symbol.

   Rev., in incuse, in early Brāhmī, *Phagunimitrasa* "(Coin) of Phalgunimitra"; above 3 symbols.

5. Taxila; double die coin. Æ. Wt. about 180 grs.

   Obv., elephant to right, above a chaitya.

   Rev., in incuse, lion standing to left, above swastika, to left chaitya.

6. Eraṇ; punch-marked. Æ.

   Obv., various symbols, including an elephant and the Ujjain symbol.

7. Andhra: Gotamīputra Viḷivāya kura. Bil. Wt. about 200 grs.

   Obv., chaitya within railing, above swastika, to right a tree.

   Rev., bow and arrow; around *Raño Gotamiputasa Viḷivāyakurasa* "(Coin) of Rāja Gotamīputra Viḷivāyakura."

8. Mathurā; Rājuvala, satrap. Bil. Wt. 38 grs.

   Obv., diademed bust of king to right; corrupt Greek legend.

   Rev., Pallas with ægis and thunderbolt to left; Kharoshṭhī legend, *Apratihatachakrasa chhatrapasa Rajavulasa* "(Coin) of the satrap Rājavula, invincible with the discus." Kharoshṭhī letters in field.

Note.—Where it has been impossible to ascertain the weight of the particular coin illustrated, the average weight of coins of its class has been given; all such weights are qualified by the word "about."

PLATE I

Plate II

KEY TO PLATE II

1. Sophytes (Saubhūti). AR. Drachm. Wt. 58·3 grs.

   Obv., helmeted head of king to right.

   Rev., cock to right, above caduceus; in Greek, *Sophutou*.

2. Pantaleon. Æ. Wt. about 160 grs.

   Obv., in incuse, lion to right. In Greek, *Basileōs Pantaleontos* "(Coin) of king Pantaleon."[1]

   Rev., Indian dancing girl. In Brāhmī, *Rajane Patalevasha*.

3. Apollodotos. Æ. Wt. 235-255 grs.

   Obv., Apollo clad in chlamys and boots standing to right, holding an arrow. In Greek, *Basileōs sōtēros Apollodotou*; monogram to left.

   Rev., tripod, Kharoshṭhī letters in field. In Kharoshṭhī, *Maharajasa tratarasa Apaladatasa* "(Coin) of the king, the saviour, Apollodotos."

4. Menander. AR. Hemidrachm. Wt. 37·7 grs.

   Obv., diademed bust of king to left, thrusting javelin with right hand. In Greek as No. 3, but *Menandrou*.

   Rev., Pallas to left with ægis on outstretched arm, hurling thunderbolt with right hand. Monogram to right. In Kharoshṭhī as No. 3, but *Menadrasa*.

5. Hippostratos. AR. Didrachm. Wt. 143·2 grs.

   Obv., diademed head of king to right. In Greek, *Basileōs megalou sōtēros Hippostratou* "(Coin) of the great king, the saviour H."

   Rev., king in full panoply on horse to right, monogram to right. In Kharoshṭhī, *Maharajasa tratarasa mahatasa jayaṁtasa Hipustratasa* "(Coin) of the king, the great saviour, the conqueror Hippostratos."

6. Menander. Æ. Wt. 38 grs.

   Obv., elephant's head with bell round neck.

   Rev., club of Herakles with two symbols.

   Legends as No. 4.

7. Philoxenos. AR. Hemidrachm. Wt. 27·3 grs.

   Obv., helmeted bust of king to right. In Greek, *Basileōs anīkētou Philoxenou*.

   Rev., king on horseback; to right, Greek letter S, and monogram. In Kharoshṭhī, *Maharajasa apaḍihatasa Philasinasa* "(Coin) of the unconquered king Philoxenos."

8. Antialkidas. AR. Hemidrachm. Wt. 37·9 grs.

   Obv., bust of king to right wearing flat "kausia." In Greek, *Basileōs nīkēphorou Antialkidou*.

   Rev., Zeus on throne bearing Nikē on outstretched right hand; elephant, retiring to left, has snatched away her crown. Monogram in field. In Kharoshṭhī, *Maharajasa jayadharasa Aṁtialikitasa*. "(Coin) of the victorious king, Antialkidas."

9. Hermaios and Kalliope. AR. Hemidrachm.

   Obv., conjugate busts of king and queen to right; in Greek, *Basileōs sōtēros Hermaiou kai Kalliopēs*.

   Rev., king on prancing horse to right. Monogram below. In Kharoshṭhī, *Maharajasa tratarasa Heramayasa Kaliyapaya*.

10. Strato I with Strato II. AR. Hemidrachm. Wt. 37 grs.

    Obv., diademed bust of aged king. In Greek, *Basileōs Sōtēros Strātōnos uiou Strātōnos*. (Meaning doubtful.)

    Rev., Pallas to left with ægis and thunderbolt. In Kharoshṭhī, *Maharajasa tratarasa Stratasa potrasa chasa priyapita Stratasa*, "(Coin) of king Strato Sōtēr and of his grandson, Strato Philopatēr."

11. Nahapāna. AR. Hemidrachm. Wt. 29·2 grs.

    Obv., head of satrap to right. Corrupt Greek legend.

    Rev., thunderbolt and arrow. In Brāhmī, *Raño Chhaharatasa*; in Kharoshṭhī, *Nahapanasa*, "(Coin) of the Kshaharāta king Nahapāna.

[1] In these bilingual coins, unless otherwise noted, the same inscription is reproduced in both languages. Technically the reverse of this coin is the obverse, as being the impression from the lower die.

KEY TO PLATE III

1. Andhra: Gotamiputra Śrī Yajña Sātakarṇi, AR. Hemidrachm. Wt. 34 grs.

   Obv., head of king to right. In Brāhmī, *Raño Gotamiputasa Siri Yaña Sātakaṇisa.*

   Rev., Ujjain symbol and chaitya. In Southern Brāhmī, *Gotam (a) putasha Hiru Yaña Hātakaṇisha* (Hiru = Śrī).

2. Western Kshatrapa: Dāmasena. AR. Wt. 34 grs.

   Obv., head of Satrap to right. Corrupt Greek inscription. Date 100 + 50 + 3 to left.

   Rev., chaitya, star and crescent. In Brāhmī, *Raño Mahākshatrapasa Rudrasīhasa putrasa raño Mahākshatrapasa Dāmasenasa* "(Coin) of king Dāmasena, the great satrap, son of king Rudrasiṁha, the great satrap."

3. Odumbara: Dharaghosha. AR. Wt. 37·5 grs.

   Obv., standing figure of Viśvāmitra(?). In Brāhmī, *Mahadevasa Raña Dharughoshasa Odumbarisa,* "(Coin) of the Mahadeva, king Dharughosha of Odumbara"; across, in Kharoshṭhī, *Viśvamitra.*

   Rev., trident, battle-axe and tree within railing. Brāhmī legend as on obverse.

4. Maues. Æ. Wt. about 130 grs.

   Obv., head of elephant to right, bell suspended from neck.

   Rev., caduceus and monogram. In Greek, *Basileōs Mauou* "(Coin) of king Maues."

5 Azes. Æ. Wt. about 220 grs.

   Obv., humped bull to right, monogram above. In Greek, *Basileōs basileōn megalou Azou.*

   Rev., in Kharoshṭhī, *Maharajasa rajatirajasa mahatasa Ayasa* "(Coin) of the great king of kings, Azes."

6. Nameless king: Sotēr Megas, Æ.

   Obv., diademed and radiate bust of king to right holding a lance: king's special symbol to left.

   Rev., king on horseback to right, symbol to right. In Greek, *Basileus basileōn sotēr megas,* "King of kings, the great saviour."

7. Azes I. AR. Didrachm. Wt. 142 grs.

   Obv., king on horseback to right, holding couched lance. Kharoshṭhī letter "Sa" below. Legend as on No. 5.

8. Gondopharnes. AR (base). Didrachm. Wt. 142 grs.

   Obv., king on horseback to right, right arm extended; king's special symbol to right. In Greek, *Basileōs basileōn megalou Undopherou.*

   Rev., Zeus standing to right, right arm extended; monogram to right, Kharoshṭhī letters to left. In Kharoshṭhī, *Maharaja rajatiraja tratara devavrada Gudupharasa,* "The king of kings, the great Gondopharnes, devoted to the gods."

9. Azilises. AR. Didrachm.

   Obv., king on horseback holding elephant-goad in right hand, symbol to right. In Greek as on No. 5, but *Azilisou.*

   Rev., Discouroi standing side by side, armed with spears. Legend as No. 5, but *Ayilishasa.*

10. Spalyris with Spalagadames. Æ.

   Obv., in square frame the king on horseback. In Greek, *Spalurios dikaiou adelphou tou basileōs* "(Coin) of Spalyris the just, the brother of the king."

   Rev., naked diademed Herakles, with club, sitting on a rock; monogram to left. In Kharoshṭhī, *Śpalahoraputrasa dhramiasa Śpalagadamasa* "(Coin) of Śpalagadames, son of Śpalahores (Spalyris) the just"

PLATE III

PLATE IV

KEY TO PLATE IV

1. Hermaios and Kujūla Kadphises. Æ.

   Obv., diademed bust of king to right. In Greek, *Basileōs stērossu Hermaiou.* (Meaning obscure.)

   Rev., Herakles facing, with lion's skin and club. In Kharoshṭhī, *Kujula Kasasa Kushana yavugasa dhramaṭhidasa* "(Coin) of Kujula Kasa, chief of the Kushāṇas, steadfast in the law."

2. Kujūla Kadaphes—imitation of a Roman type. Æ.

   Obv., diademed head to right. In corrupt Greek, *Khoranou zaoou Kozola Kadaphes.*

   Rev., king seated to right on a chair, behind him a monogram. In Kharoshṭhī, . . . *Kaphsasa*[1] *sachadhramaṭhitasa Khushanasa yüasa* "(Coin) of Kapsha, chief of the Kushāṇas, steadfast in the true law."

3. Vima Kadphises. AV. Double stater. Wt. 244·2 grs.

   Obv., king seated cross-legged, wearing crested helmet and diadem, thunderbolt in right hand; symbol to left. Legend in Greek letters, *Basileus Ooemo Kadphises.*

   Rev., Śiva radiate, standing in front of bull, long trident in right hand; symbol to left. In Kharoshṭhī, *Maharajasa rajadhirajasa sarvaloga iśvarasa Mahiśvarasa Vima Kaṭhphiśasa tradara* "(Coin) of the great king, the king of kings, lord of the world, the Maheśvara, Vima Kaṭhphiśa, the defender."[2]

4. Kanishka. AV. Wt. 122 grs.

   Obv., king radiate, standing to left sacrificing at a small altar, spear in left hand. In Greek characters, *Shāonānoshāo Kaneshki Koshāno* "(Coin) of the king of kings, Kanishka the Kushāṇa."

   Rev., Buddha facing nimbate, wallet in left hand; to right symbol. In Greek, *Boddo.*

5. Kanishka. AV. Wt. 30·8 grs.

   Obv., half-length portrait of king to left, spear in left hand. Legend as on No. 4.

   Rev., bearded deity to left, with fillet in right hand and tongs in left. To left symbol, to right *Athsho.*

6. Kanishka. Æ.

   Obv., as No. 4, but legend *Shāo Kaneshki.*

   Rev., Wind-god, undraped and radiate, running to left; to left symbol, to right *Oado.*

7. Huvishka. AV. Wt. 120·9 grs.

   Obv., king riding on an elephant to right, holds sceptre and elephant-goad. Legend as on No. 4, but *Oēshki.*

   Rev., goddess to right, holding cornucopiae in both hands; to right symbol, to left *Ardokhsho.*

8. Huvishka. AV. Wt. 123 grs.

   Obv., king seated cross-legged, turning to left; goad in left hand, sceptre in right. Legend as on No. 7.

   Rev., bearded Herakles, with club and lion's skin, standing, apple in left hand; to left symbol, to right *Herakilo.*

9. Vasudeva. AV. Wt. 122·3 grs.

   Obv., similar to No. 4, but king wears suit of chain-mail; also name *Bazodēo* in legend.

   Rev., many-headed Śiva, standing in front of bull, trident in left hand; symbol to right, to left *Oesho.*

10. Later Great Kushāṇa. AV. Wt. 121·4 grs.

    Obv., as No. 4, but corrupt legend, Nāgarī letters, to left "ha," to right "vi."

    Rev., goddess seated on throne facing, holding noose in right, cornucopiae in left hand; left, above symbol, below Nāgarī "la"; to right *Ardokhsho.*

11. Yaudheya. Æ.

    Obv., soldier standing, holding spear in right hand. In Brāhmī, *Yaudheyagaṇasya iaya dvi* . . . "Of the clan of Yaudheyas (?)"

    Rev., standing figure, symbol on either side.

[1] Four different Kharoshṭhī forms appear on coins—Kasa, Kaphsa, Kadapha and Kaü. It is uncertain how many persons they denote.

[2] Maheśvara (Mahesh) is a name of Śiva.

KEY TO PLATE V

1. Nepāl: Aṁśuvarman. Æ.
   Obv., cow to left, *Kāmadehī*, "The cow that yields every wish."
   Rev., winged lion to left, *Śryaṁśuvarma*.
2. Samudragupta. Standard type. AV. Wt. 116 grs.
   Obv., king standing to left, holding standard in left hand, sacrificing at altar to his right; behind altar Garuḍa-headed standard; beneath king's arm, *Samudra*; around, *Samaraśatavitatavijayo jitaripur ajito divaṁ jayati*, "The unconquered one, whose victories extend over a century of battles, having conquered his enemies, wins heaven."
   Rev., goddess Lakshmī on a throne, her feet on a lotus; to left symbol, to right *Parākramaḥ*, "The [king] of supreme might."
3. Id: Lyrist type. AV. Wt. 119·5 grs.
   Obv., king seated cross-legged on high-backed couch, playing on a lyre; beneath couch a foot-stool inscribed *Si*. Legend, *Mahārājādhirāja Śrī Samudraguptaḥ*.
   Rev., Lakshmī seated on wicker stool, holding fillet in right hand, cornucopiae on left arm; to right *Samudraguptaḥ*.
4. Id: Chandragupta I type. AV. Wt. 118 grs.
   Obv., Chandragupta on right, holding crescent-topped standard, offering ring to Kumāradevī on left; on right *Chandragupta*; on left *Śrī Kumāradevī*.
5. Id: Aśvamedha type. AV. Wt. 118·6 grs.
   Obv., horse stands to left before a sacrificial post; beneath horse *Si*; around, parts of *Rājādhirājaḥ prithivīvijitva divaṁ jayatyā hṛtavājimedhaḥ*, "The king of kings, having conquered the earth, wins heaven, being the restorer of the Aśvamedha."
6. Chandragupta II. Archer type. AV. Wt. 124·3 grs.
   Obv., king standing to left, drawing arrow from a quiver; Garuḍa standard on left; under left arm, *Chandra*; around, *Deva Śrī Mahārājādhirāja Śrī Chandraguptaḥ*.
   Rev., goddess seated facing, on lotus; lotus in left, fillet in right hand; symbol to left; to right, *Śrī Vikrama*.
7. Id: Chattra type. AV. Wt. 119 grs.
   Obv., king standing to left, casting incense on altar; behind him dwarf attendant holds a "chattra" over his head. Around, *Kṣitim avajitya sucaritair divaṁ jayati Vikramādityaḥ*, "Vikramāditya, having conquered the earth, wins heaven by good deeds."
   Rev., goddess Lakshmī standing facing, holding fillet and lotus; symbol to left; to right, *Vikramādityaḥ*.
8. Id: Horseman type. AV. Wt. 120·7 grs.
   Obv., king riding on fully caparisoned horse to left, holding a bow. Around, *Paramabhāgavata Mahārājādhirāja Śrī Chandraguptaḥ*, "Supreme among Bhāgavatas, king of kings," etc.
   Rev., as No. 3. To right, *Ajitavikramaḥ*, "He whose prowess is unsurpassed."
9. Kumāragupta I. Lion-slayer type. AV. Wt. 125·6 grs.
   Obv., king standing to right shoots a lion, which falls backward. Around, *Kumāragupto yudhi siṅhavikkramaḥ*, "Kumāragupta, who has the valour of a lion in battle."
   Rev., goddess Ambikā-Lakshmī seated facing, on a lion, holding fillet and lotus. To right, *Siṅhamahendraḥ*, "The lion Mahendra."
10. Id: Peacock type. AV. Wt. 128·5 grs.
    Obv., king standing to left, feeding peacock with a bunch of grapes. Legend uncertain.
    Rev., Karttikeya, riding on his peacock, Parvāṇi, spear in left hand, sprinkling incense on altar. To right, *Mahendrakumāraḥ*.
11. Prakāśāditya. Horseman type. AV. Wt. 145·1 grs.
    Obv., king slaying a lion from horseback; Garuḍa standard on right. Legend incomplete.
    Rev., goddess seated as on No. 6. To right, *Śrī Prakāśāditya*.
12. Śaśāṅka, king of Gauḍa. AV. Wt. 145 grs.
    Obv., Śiva nimbate, reclining on bull (Nandi); moon above on left. On right, *Śrī Śa*; below, *jaya*.
    Rev., Lakshmī seated on lotus, elephants above on either side sprinkling water on her. On right, *Śrī Śaśāṅka*.
13. Chandragupta II. Chattra type. Æ.
    Obv., as on No. 7.
    Rev., Garuḍa standing facing, with outspread wings and human arms. Below, portions of *Mahārāja Śrī Chandraguptaḥ*.

PLATE V

PLATE VI

KEY TO PLATE VI

1. Kumāragupta I. W. Provinces type. AR. Wt. 33·5 grs.
   Obv., bust of king to right; corrupt Greek letters.
   Rev., Garuḍa standing facing, with outstretched wings. Around, *Paramabhāgavata Mahārājādhirāja Śrī Kumāragupta Mahendrādityaḥ.*

2. Skandagupta. Central Provinces Type. AR. Wt. 32·1 grs.
   Obv., bust of king to right; to right, date in Brāhmī numerals.
   Rev., peacock standing facing, with wings and tail outspread; border of dots. Around, *Vijitāvanir avanipati jayati divaṁ Skandagupto 'yam*, "This Skandagupta, having conquered the world, [as] world-lord, wins heaven."

3. Śilāditya (Harshavardhana) of Thāṇeśar. AR. Wt. about 36 grs.
   Obv., bust of king to left; to left, *Sa* and uncertain date.
   Rev., peacock as on No. 2. Around, *Vijitāvanir avanipati. Śrī Śilāditya divaṁ jayati*, "Śrī Śilāditya having conquered the world, [as] world-lord, wins heaven."

4. Mihiragula. AR. Wt. 54·2 grs.
   Obv., bust of king to right; in front, bull-standard; behind, trident. Legend, *Jayatu Mihirakula.*
   Rev., debased fire-altar and attendants.

5. Napki Malik. AR (base). About 52 grs.
   Obv., bust of king with winged head-dress; above, buffalo's head facing. Pahlavi legend, *Napkī Malik.*
   Rev., Fire-altar and attendants, wheel over head of each.

6. Indian imitation of Sassanian coin. AR (base).
   Obv, and Rev., as on No. 4, but very barbarous.

7. Toramāṇa. AR. Wt. 32·8 grs.
   Obv., as on No. 3.
   Rev., as on No. 3, but *Śrī Toramāṇa.*

8. Gadhiya paisa. AR (base). Wt. 60 grs.
   Obv., head of king to right.
   Rev., fire-altar. More debased than No. 6.

9. Mahoba: Hallakshaṇavarma. AV. Dramma. Wt. 63 grs.
   Obv., four-armed goddess seated facing.
   Rev., *Śrīmad Hallakshaṇavarma Deva.*

10. Ḍahāla: Gāṅgeya-deva. AV. Wt. 62 grs.
    Obv., as on No. 9.
    Rev., *Śrīmad Gāṅgeya deva.*

11. Dehlī and Ajmer: Pṛithvī Rājā. Bil. Wt. 52 grs.
    Obv., horseman to right; *Śrī Pṛithvī Rājā deva.*
    Rev., recumbent bull to left; *Asāvari Śrī Sāmanta deva.*[1]

12. Shāhīs of Ohind: Spalapati-deva. AR. Wt. 50 grs.
    Obv., horseman to right. Inscription in undeciphered characters.
    Rev., recumbent bull to left. *Śrī Spalapati deva.*

13. Narwar: Chāhaḍa-deva. Æ. Wt. 52 grs.
    Obv., as No. 11, but legend *Śrī Chāhaḍa deva.*
    Rev., as No. 11.

14. Kashmīr; Harsha-deva. AV. Wt. 73 grs.
    Obv., horseman to right; *Harsha deva.*
    Rev., seated goddess.

15. Id: Diddā Rānī. Æ. Wt. about 85 grs.
    Obv., standing king to right.
    Rev., seated goddess. To left, *Śrī*; to right, *Diddā.*

16. Id: Yaśovarman. AV (base). Wt. 112 grs.
    Obv., standing king; under left arm, *Kidā (ra).*
    Rev., seated goddess, *Śrī Yaśovarma.*

[1] Asāvari is said to be a name of Durga; Śrī Sāmanta deva is borrowed from the coinage of Ohind.

KEY TO PLATE VII

1. Gold globule, with faint punch-mark on reverse. Wt. about 52 grs.

2. Padma-ṭaṅka. AV. Wt. 57 grs.

   Obv., eight-petalled lotus, surrounded by "Śaṅka" and two other symbols. Inscription in a form of Nāgarī.

3. Pāṇḍya. AV. Wt. 57 grs.

   Obv., two fishes under canopy; to right, lamp, to left, "chauri" (fly-whisk).

   Rev., undeciphered inscription.

4. Eastern Chālukya: Rājarāja. AV. Wt. 66·8 grs.

   Obv., in centre, boar to right; around, *Śrī Rājarāja Sa* (*ṁvat*) *35*.

5. Koṅgudeśa. AV. Wt. 60·2 grs.

   Obv., ornate elephant to right.

   Rev., floral scroll design.

6. Choḷa. AR. Wt. 52 grs.

   Obv. and Rev., tiger seated under a canopy, behind it a bow, in front two fish, whole flanked by two fly-whisks. In Nāgarī, below, *Śrī Rājendraḥ*.

7. Ceylon: Parākrama Bāhu. Æ.

   Obv., standing king.

   Rev., seated goddess. In Nāgarī, *Śrī Parākramabāhu*.

8. Pallava or Chālukya (?). AR. Wt. 103·9 grs.

   Obv., lion to right.

   Rev., vase on stand, circle of rays.

9. Kerala. AR. Wt. 36·3 grs.

   Obv., undeciphered inscription.

   Rev., in Nāgarī, *Śrī Vīrakeralasya*.

10. Kalikūt: Tipū. AV. Fanam. Wt. about 5·2 grs.

    Obv., Persian "hē" (= Ḥaidar).

    Rev., in Persian, *Kalīkūt, 1199*.

11. Vijayanagar: Kṛishṇa Deva Rāya. AV. Half pagoda. Wt. about 26 grs.

    Obv., Vishṇu seated with discus and conch.

    Rev., in Nāgarī, *Śrī Pratāpa Kṛishṇa Rāya*.

12. Id: Harihara II. AV. Half pagoda. Wt. 25 grs.

    Obv., god and goddess seated.

    Rev., in Nāgarī, *Śrī Pratāpa Harihara*.

13. Kananūr: 'Alī Rāja. AV.

    Obv., in Arabic, *Al-wālīu-l-mulk 'Alī Rājā*, "The guardian of the kingdom, 'Alī Rājā."

    Rev., *Bi-l-hijrati as-sina 1194*, "In the Hijri year 1194."

PLATE VII

PLATE VIII

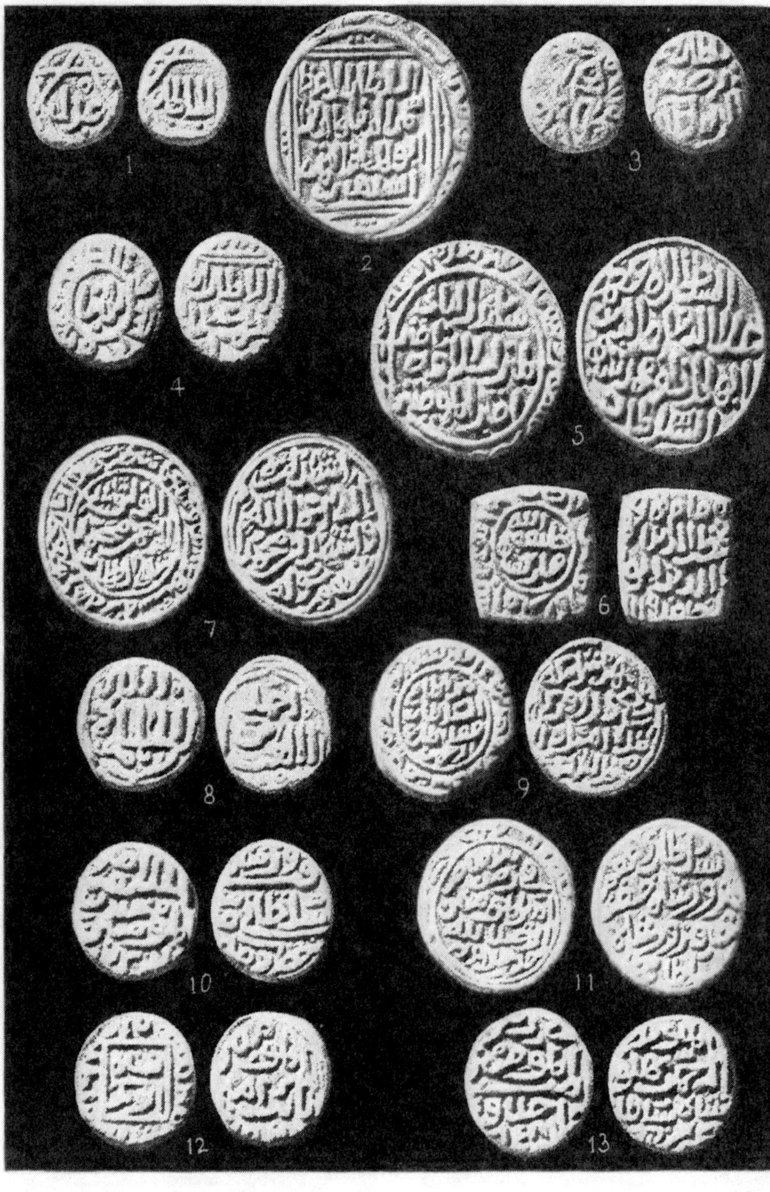

Key to Plate VIII

1. Altamsh. Æ.
   Obv., in hexagon, *'Adl.*
   Rev., in square, inscribed in a circle, *As-sulṭān.*

2. Id: AR. Wt. about 165 grs.
   Rev., in square, inscribed in a circle, *As-sulṭānu-l-a'ẓam Shamsu-d-dunyā wa-d-dīn abu-l-muẓaffar Altamsh as-sulṭān,* "The supreme sultan, the sun of the world and the faith, the father of the victorious, Altamsh the sultan." Marginal legends incomplete.

3. Raẓiya. Bil. Wt. about 54 grs.
   Obv., horseman to right. Around, in Nāgarī, *Śrī Hamīrah* (=the Amīr).
   Rev., in Arabic, *As-sulṭānu-l-a'ẓam Raẓiyatu-d-dunyā wa-d-dīn.*

4. Ghiyāṣu-d-dīn Balban. Bil. Wt. about 55 grs.
   Obv., in circle, in Arabic, *Balban*; around, in Nāgarī, *Śrī Sultān Giyāsudīn.*
   Rev., in Arabic, *As-sulṭānu-l-a'ẓam Ghiyāṣu-d-dunyā wa-d-dīn.*

5. 'Alāu-d-dīn Muḥammad. Dehlī. 698 A.H. AV. Wt. 170 grs.
   Obv., in a circle, *Sikandaru-ṣ-ṣānī yamīnu-l-khilāfati nāṣiru amīru-l-mominīn,* "The second Alexander, the right hand of the Khalifate, the helper of the commander of the faithful"; margin, *Ẓuriba hazihi-s-sikkatu bi ḥaẓrati Dehlī fī sinate ṣamāna wa tis 'aina wa sittami 'ata,* "Struck this coin at the capital, Dehlī, in the year eight and ninety and six hundred."
   Rev., as on No. 2, but title, *'Alāu-d-dunyā wa-d-dīn,* and name *Muḥammad Shāh.*

6. Quṭbu-d-dīn Mubārak. 719 A.H. Bil. Wt. 80 grs.
   Obv., in circle, *Khalīfatu 'llah Mubārak Shāh,* "The Khalif of God, Mubārak Shāh"; around, *As-sulṭan al wāṣiqu bi' llah amīru-l-mominīn,* "The sultan, the truster in God, the commander of the faithful."
   Rev., *Al imāmu-l-a'ẓam Quṭbu-d-dunyā wa-d-dīn abu-l-muẓaffar,* "The Supreme Imām, Quṭbu-d-dīn, the father of the victorious."

7. Muḥammad bin Tughlaq. Dehlī. 726 AH. A.V. Wt. 199 grs.
   Obv., in circle, *Al wāṣiqu bi ta'īdu-r-rahman* ("The truster in the help of the Merciful") *Muhammad Shāh as-sulṭān.* Margin similar to that on No. 5, but *hazihi-d-dīnār* and date 726 in Arabic words.
   Rev., *Ashhadu an lā ilāha illallaho wa ashhadu an Muḥammadan 'abduhu wa rasūluhu,* "I testify that there is no god but God, and I testify that Muḥammad is his servant and apostle."

8. Id: in the name of the Khalif Al Ḥākim. Bil. Wt. about 140 grs.
   Obv., within quatrefoil, *Al Ḥākim b' amru'llah.*
   Rev., within quatrefoil, *Abu-l-'abbās Aḥmad.*

9. Id: Forced Currency. Tughlaqpūr, 730 AH. Brass. Wt. about 140 grs.
   Obv., in circle, *Man atā' as-sulṭān faqad atā' ar-rahmān,* "He who obeys the sultan surely he obeys the Merciful"; margin, in Persian, *Dar iqlīm-i-Tughlaqpūr 'urf Tirhut sāl bar hafsad sī* "(Struck) in the territory of Tulghlaqpūr, alias Tirhut, in the year seven hundred and thirty."
   Rev., in Persian, *Muhar shud tankah-i-ra'īj dar rūzgāh-i-bandah-i-ummīdwār Muḥammad Tughlaq,* "Stamped as a tankah current in the reign of the slave, hopeful (of mercy), Muḥammad Tughlaq."

10. Fīroz Shāh. Dehlī. 773 A.H. Bil. Wt. 140 grs.
   Obv., *Al Khalīfatu amiru-l-mominīn khuldat khilāfatuhu 773,* "The Khalif of the Commander of the faithful, may the Khalifate be perpetuated."
   Rev., *Fīroz Shāh sulṭānī ẓuriba bi ḥaẓrati Dehlī,* cf. No. 5, Obv., margin.

11. Fīroz Shāh Ẓafar. AV. Wt. 169 grs.
   Obv., in circle, *Fī zamani-l-imāmi amīru-l-mominīn Abu 'Abdu-'llah khuldat khilāfatuhu,* "In the time of the Imām, the commander of the faithful, Abu 'Abd-ullah," etc.; margin illegible.
   Rev., *As-sulṭānu-l-a'ẓam Fīroz Shāh Ẓafar Shāh ibn-i-Fīroz Shāh sulṭānī,* "The supreme sultan, Fīroz Shāh Ẓafar Shāh, son of Fīroz Shāh, sultan."

12. Abūbakr Shāh. 792 A.H. Æ. Wt. about 102 grs.
   Obv., in square, *Abūbakr Shāh*; in margin, *bin Ẓafar bin Fīroz Shāh sulṭānī.*
   Rev., *Nā'ibi amīru-l-mominīn 792,* "The deputy of the Commander of the faithful."

13. Bahlol Lodī. Dehlī. 858 A.H. Bil. Wt. 140-146 grs.
   Obv., *Fī zamani amīru-l-mominīn khuldat khilāfatuhu 858.*
   Rev., *Al mutawakkilu 'ala-r-rahmān* ("Trusting in the Merciful one") *Bahlol Shāh sulṭān bi ḥaẓrati Dehlī.*

Key to Plate IX

1. Bengal: Sikandar Shāh. Firozābād. 783 A.H. AR. Wt. 166 grs.

Obv., in a circle, *Abu-l-mujāhid* ("The father of the warrior") *Sikandar Shāh ibn-i-Ilyās Shāh sulṭān*; margin, names of the Four Companions in four circles, between these *Al imāmu-l-a'ẓamu-l-wāṣiqu bi ta'īdu-r-rahman*; cf. Pl. VIII, 7, Obv.

Rev., *Yamīni Khalīfatu'llah naṣīru amīru-l-mominīn ghauṣu-l-islām wa-l-muslimīn khallada mulkahu*, "The right hand of the Khalif of God, the helper of the Commander of the faithful, the succourer of Islām and the Muslims, may God perpetuate the kingdom"; margin, in segments, *Ẓuriba hazihi-s-sikkatu-l-mubārikatu fī baldati Fīrozābād*, "Struck this blessed coin in the town of Fīrozābād," followed by date 783 in Arabic words.

2. Bahmanī: 'Alāu-d-dīn Aḥmad II. 850 A.H. AR. Wt. 169 grs.

Obv., *As-sulṭānu-l-ḥalīm ul karīm ur ra'ufi 'alai 'abdu'llah al ghanīu-l-muhaimin*, "The sultan, the clement, the bountiful, the kind to the servants of God, the rich, the confiding one."

Rev., in a square, *Abu-l-muzaffar 'Alāu-d-dunyā wa-d-dīn Āḥmad Shāh bin Aḥmad Shāh al wālīu-l-bahmanī* ("The guardian, the Bahmanī").

3. Mālwā: Ghiyāṣ Shāh. 880 A.H. AV. Wt. 170 grs.

Obv., in double square, the outer one dotted, *Al wāṣiqu b'il mulki al multaji abu-l-fatḥ* ("The truster in the kingdom, and seeking refuge in the Father of victory") *Ghiyāṣ Shāh*. A star above.

Rev., *Bin Maḥmūd Shāh sulṭānu-l-Khiljī khallada mulkahu 880.*

4. Jaunpūr: Maḥmūd Shāh. 846 (?) A.H. AV. Wt. 175 grs.

Obv., within circle, *Fī zamani-l-imāmi nā'ībi amīru-l-mominīn abu-l-fatḥ khuldat khilāfatuhu.* Cf. Pl. VIII, 11. Margin, as on Pl. VIII, 5, but date 846 (?) and mint name missing.

Rev., in tughra characters, *As-sulṭān ṣaifu-d-dunyā wa-d-dīn abu-l-mujāhid Maḥmūd bin Ibrāhīm.*

5. Id: Ḥusain Shāh. 864 AH. Æ. Wt. 150 grs.

Obv., in circle, *Ḥusain Shāh*; margin, *bin Maḥmūd Shāh bin Ibrāhīm Shāh sulṭānī.*

Rev., *Nā'ībi amīru-l-mominīn 864.*

6. Gujarāt: Maḥmūd Shāh III 946. AH. AV. Wt. 185 grs.

Obv., reading upwards, *Nāṣiru-d-dunyā wa-d-dīn abu-l-fatḥ al wāṣiqu bi'llahi-i-mannān*, "The helper of the world and the faith, the father of victory, the truster in the beneficent God."

Rev., in double square, *Maḥmūd Shāh bin Laṭīf Shāh sulṭān*; margin, *946.*

7. Id: Maḥmūd Shāh III. AR. Wt. 112 grs.

Obv. and Rev., legends as No. 6, but no date.

8. Ma'bar: 'Ādil Shāh. Æ.

Obv., *As-sulṭān 'Ādil Shāh.*

Rev., *As-sulṭānu-l-a'ẓam.*

9. Kashmir: Zainu-l-'ābidin. 842 A.H. AR. Wt. 96 grs.

Obv., *As-sulṭānu-l-a'ẓam Zainu-l-'ābidīn 842.*

Rev., in lozenge, *Ẓuriba Kashmīr*; in marginal segments, *Fī shuhūri sina iṣnai wa arb'aina wa ṣamanami'ata*, "In the months of the year two and forty and eight hundred."

10. Bījāpūr: 'Ādil Shāh. Lārin. Wt. about 71 grs.

Obv., *'Ādil Shāh*, followed by 3 strokes.

Rev., blurred.

Plate IX

PLATE X

KEY TO PLATE X

1. Bābur: Lāhor. 936 AH. AR. Wt. 69 grs.

Obv., in circle, the Kalima; margin, in segments, portions of *Abābakri-ṣ-ṣadīq* ("A, the faithful witness"), *'Umru-l-fārūq* ("'U, the discriminator between right and wrong"), *'Uṣmān abu Nūrain* ("'U, the father of two lights") *'Alīu-l-murtaẓa* ("'A, the pleasing to God").

Rev., within flattened mihrabi area, *Ẓahīru-d-dīn Muḥammad Bābur bādshāh ghāzī, 936*; above, *As-sulṭānu-l-a'ẓamu-l-khāqānu-mukarram*, "The most great sultan, the illustrious emperor"; below, *Khallada allaha ta'ālā mulkahu wa salṭanatuhu*, "May God Most High perpetuate the kingdom and sovereignity" and, *Ẓuriba Lāhor* "Struck at Lāhor."

2. Humāyūn. AV. Wt. 16 grs.

Obv., in circle, the Kalima.

Rev., *Khallada allaha ta'ālā mulkahu. . . . . Muḥammad Humāyūn bādshāh ghāzī.*

3. Sher Shāh. Āgra. 948 A.H. AR. Wt. 175 grs.

Obv., in square, the Kalima; margins as on No. 1.

Rev., in square, *Sher Shāh sulṭān khallada allāhu mulkahu 948*; below in Nāgarī, *Śrī Śēr Sāhi* (an attempt at Sher Shāh's name).

Margins, *As-sulṭānu-l-'ādil abu-l-muẓaffar* ("The just sultan, the father of the victorious") *Farīdu-d-dīn ẓuriba Āgrah.*

4. Islām Shāh. Qanauj. 95—. Æ. Wt. 315 grs.

Obv., *Fī 'ahdi-l-amīru-l-ḥāmiu-d-dīni wa-d-dayān 95*—"In the time of the prince, the defender of the faith of the requiter." Double bar, with knot in centre, bisects the legend.

Rev., *Abu-l-muẓaffar Islām Shāh bin Sher Shāh sulṭān ẓuriba Shergarh 'urf Qanauj khallada allāhu mulkahu*, "The father of the victorious, Islām Shāh, son of Sher Shāh, sultan, struck (this coin) at Shergarh alias Qanauj: may God perpetuate the kingdom."

5. Sikandar Sūr. 962. AR. Wt. 174 grs.

Rev., in square, *Sulṭān Sikandar Shāh Isma'īl Sūr 962.* Margins illegible.

6. Akbar. Āgra. 981. AV. Wt. 167 grs.

Obv., in dotted border, the Kalima. Names of the four companions and *981.*

Rev., *Khallada mulkahu Jalālu-d-dīn Muḥammad Akbar bādshāh ghāzī ẓuriba baldatī Āgrah* ("Struck at Āgra town").

7. Id: Aḥmadābād. 982. AR. Wt 175 grs.

Rev., within dotted square border, *Jalālu-d-dīn Muḥammad Akbar bādshāh ghāzī, 982*; margins, portions of *As-sulṭānu-l-a'ẓam khallada allāhu ta'ālā mulkahu wa salṭanatahu ẓuriba daru-s-salṭanati Aḥmadābād* ("Struck at the seat of sovereignty Aḥmadābād").

8. Id: Āgra.[1] 50 R. AR. Wt. 175 grs.

Obv., in octagonal border, on ornamental ground, *Allāhu Akbar jalla jalālahu*, "God is great, eminent is his glory."

Rev., within similar border, *Ẓarb-i-Āgrah Amardād Ilāhī 50*, "Struck at Āgra, Amardād Ilāhī year 50."

9. Id: Āgra. [50 R.] AV. Wt. 182 grs.

Obv., within dotted circle, on ornamented ground, a duck to right.

10. Id: Dehlī. 43 R. Æ. Wt. about 640 grs.

Obv., *Tankah-i-Akbar Shāhī ẓarb-i-Dehlī*, Tankah of Akbar Shāh, struck at Dehlī."

Rev., *Māh Dī Ilāhī 43*, "In the month Dī, Ilāhī year 43."

11. Id: Mintless. 43 R. AR. Wt. 87, grs. Half rupee.

Obv., within square dotted border, legend as on No. 8.

Rev., *Shahrīwar Ilāhī 43.*

12. Jahāngīr. 1014-1 R. AR. (A "Khair qabūl.")

Obv., within dotted border *Jahāngīr bādshāh ghāzī 1.*

Rev., *Khair qabūl*, "May these alms be accepted."

[1] With the introduction of the Ilāhī coins, Persian gradually supersedes Arabic in the inscriptions.

KEY TO PLATE XI

1. Jahāngīr. Lāhor. 1016-3 R. AR. Wt. 209 grs.

   Obv., within square border of dots, on ornamented ground, the Kalima; below, *Ẓarb-i-Lāhor 1016.*

   Rev., *Nūru-d-dīn Muḥammad Jahāngīr bādshāh g͟hāzī sana 3.*

2. Id: Āgra. 1028-14 R. AV. Wt. 168 grs.

   Obv., ram skipping to left, surmounted by sun; below, *Sana 14 julūs,* "The 14th year from the accession."

   Rev., *Yāft dar Āgrah rū-i-zar zīwar* || *Az Jahāngīr Shāh-i-Shāh Akbar,* "The face of gold received ornament at Āgra from Jahāngīr Shāh, Shāh Akbar [s. Son]," and *Sana 1028.*

3. Id: Ajmer. 1023-9 R. AV. Wt. 168 grs.

   Obv., Jahāngīr nimbate seated cross-legged on throne, head to left, goblet in right hand. Around, *Qaẓā bar sikka-i-zar kard taṣwīr* || *Shabīh-i-ḥaẓrat-i-Shāh-i-Jahāngīr,* "Destiny on coin of gold has drawn the portrait of His Majesty Shāh Jahāngīr."

   Rev., sun in square compartment in centre; to left, *Ẓarb-i-Ajmer 1023*; to right, *Ya mu'īnu,*[1] "O thou fixed one," and *Sana 9*; above and below, *Ḥarūf-i-Jahāngīr u Allāhu Akbar* || *Zi rūz-i-azal dar 'adad shud barābar,* "The letters of Jahāngīr and 'Allāhu Akbar'[2] are equal in value from the beginning of time."

4. Id: Āgra. 1019-5 R. AR. Wt. 220 grs.

   Obv., within multifoil area on flowered ground, *Dar isfandārmuz īn sikka-rā dar Āgrah zad bar zar,* "In Isfandārmuz placed this stamp at Āgra on money," with date *5.*

   Rev., contained as obv., *Shahanshāh-i-zamān Shāh Jahāngīr ibn-i-Shāh Akbar,* "The emperor of the age, Shāh Jahāngīr, son of Akbar Shāh"; with date *1019.*

5. Id: with Nūr Jahān. Sūrat. 1036. AV. Wt. 166 grs.

   Obv., *Zi ḥukm-i-Shāh Jahāngīr yāft ṣad zīwar.*

   Rev., *Ba nām-i-Nūr Jahān Bādshāh Begam zar,*

   "By order of Shāh Jahāngīr, gained a hundred beauties gold, through the name of Nūr Jahān Bādshāh Begam"; on obv., *Ẓarb-i-Sūrat*; rev., 1036.

6. Id: in the name Salīm. Aḥmadābād. 2 R. AR. Wt. 176 grs.

   Obv., *Māliku-l-mulk sikka zad bar zar.*

   Rev., *Shāh Sulṭān Salīm Shāh Akbar,* "The Lord of the realm placed (his) stamp on money, Shāh Sultan Salīm Akbar Shāh ['S Son]"; on Obv., *Ẓarb-i-Aḥmadābād*; Rev., *Farwardīn sana 2.*

7. Shāh Jahān I. Aḥmadābād. 1038-2 R. AR. Wt. 168 grs.

   Obv., the Kalima in 3 lines; below, *Ẓarb-i-Aḥmadābād sana 2 Ilāhī māh K͟hūrdād,* "Struck at Aḥmadābād in the month K͟hūrdād of the Ilāhī year 2."

   Rev., *Ṣāḥib-i-qirān ṡānī Shihābu-d-dīn Shāh Jahān bādshāh g͟hāzī sana 1038.*

8. Id: Shāhjahānābād. 1069. AV. Niṡār. Wt. 43 grs.

   Obv., *Niṡār-i-Ṣāḥib-i-qirān ṡānī.*

   Rev., *Ẓarb-i-dāru-l-k͟hilāfat Shāhjahānābād 1069.* "Niṡār of the 'second lord of the conjunction,' struck at the capital, Shāhjahānābād, 1069."

9. Aurangzeb: Tatta. 1072-5 R. AV. Wt. 170 grs.

   Obv., *Sikka zad dar jahān chū mihr-i-munīr* || *Shāh Aurangzeb 'Ālamgīr, 1072,* "Struck money through the world like the shining sun, Shāh Aurangzeb 'Ālamgīr."

   Rev., *Ẓarb-i-Tatta sana 5 julūs-i-maimanat-i-mānūs,* "Struck at Tatta in the 5th year of the accession associated with prosperity."

10. Shāh Shujā': Akbarnagar. 1068-aḥd. AR. Wt. 177 grs.

    Obv., in square, the Kalima and 1068; in margins, names of Four Companions with epithets.

    Rev., in square, *Muḥammad Shāh Shujā' bādshāh g͟hāzī*; right margin, *Ṣāḥib-i-qirān ṡānī*; lower margin, *Akbar [nagar].*

11. Aurangzeb: Katak. 29 R. AR. Wt. about 44 grs.

    Obv., in dotted square border, on ornamental ground, *Dirham shar'ī.*

    Rev., *Ẓarb-i-Katak 29.*

[1] With a reference to K͟hwāja Mu'īnu-d-dīn Chishtī, buried at Ajmer, A.D. 1236.

[2] By the abjad system of reckoning, the letters of Jahāngīr and Allāhu Akbar both make up 288.

Note. In the Plate the reverses and obverses of Nos. 4, 6, 8 and 10 have been, by a mistake, transposed.

PLATE XI

PLATE XII

Key to Plate XII

1. Shāh ʻĀlam II. Shāhjahānābād, 1219-47 R. AV. Wt. 166 grs.
   Obv. and Rev., surrounded with circular border of roses, shamrocks and thistles.
   Obv., *Sikka-i-Ṣāḥib-i-qirānī zad zi tāʼīdu-llah* || *Ḥāmī-i-dīn-i-Muhammad Shāh ʻĀlam bādshāh*, "Struck coin like the 'lord of the conjunction,' by the help of God, Defender of the Faith, Muḥammad Shāh ʻĀlam, the king." Date *1219*; mint marks, umbrella and cinquefoil.
   Rev., as. Pl XI, No. 9, but date *47*; and mint, Shāhjahānābād.

2. Aḥmad Shāh Durrānī. Shāhjahānābād, 1170-11 R. AR. Rupee.
   Obv., *Ḥukm shud az qādir-i-bīchūn ba Aḥmad bādshāh* || *Sikka zan bar sīm u zar az auj-i-māhī tā-ba māh*, "There came an order from the potent Incomparable One to Aḥmad the king to strike coin on gold and silver from the zenith of Pisces to the Moon. Date, *1170*."
   Rev., as on No. 1, but date *11*.

3. Awadh: Wājid ʻAlī Shāh. 1264-2 R. AV. Muhar.
   Obv., arms of Awadh; around, *Ẓarb-i-mulk-i-Āwadh bailu-s-salṭanat Lakhnau sana 2 julūs-i-maimanat-i-mānūs*, "Struck in the country of Awadh, at the seat of sovereignty, Lakhnau," etc.
   Rev., *Sikka zad bar sīm u zar az faẓl-i-tāʼīdu-llah*, || *Ẓill-i-haqq Wājid ʻAlī Sulṭān-i-ʻālam bādshāh*, "Struck coin in silver and gold through the grace of the divine help, the shade of God, Wājid ʻAlī, sultan of the world, the king." Date, *2*.

4. Ḥaidarābād. Sikandar Jāh, in the name of the Mughal Akbar II. AR. Rupee.
   Obv., *Sikka-i-mubārak-i-bādshāh ghāzī Muḥammd Akbar Shāh, 1237*, "Blessed coin of the king," etc.; with initial letter "sīn" of Sikandar.
   Rev., as on No. 1, but year *16*, and mint, *Farkhanda bunyād Ḥaidarābād*, "Ḥaidarābād, of fortunate foundation."

5. Mysore. Tīpū. Seringapatam. Æ. 20 cash.
   Obv., elephant with lowered trunk to right.
   Rev., *Ẓarb-i-Pattan*.

6. Nepāl. Pṛithvī Nārāyaṇa. AR. Wt. 84 grs.
   Obv., within circle a square; above sun and moon; below date, *1691* (Śaka=A.D. 1769); at sides ornaments. In square, small circle containing trident in centre; around, in Nāgarī, *Śrī Śrī Pṛithvī Nārāyaṇa Sāhadeva*.
   Rev., within central circle, *Śrī Śrī Bhavānī*; marginal legend, each character in an ornament, *Śrī Śrī Gorakhanātha*.

7. Indore. Jaśwant Rāo. AR. Rupee.
   Obv., in Sanskrit, *Śrī Indraprasthasthito rājā chakravartī bhumaṇḍale*, || *Tatprasādat kṛitā mudrā lokesmin vai virājite*.
   Rev., *Lakshmīkāntapadāmbhojabhramara-rājitachetasaḥ*, || *Yeśawantasya vikhyātā mudraisha pṛithivītale*, "By permission of the king of Indraprastha (Dehlī), the emperor of the world, this coin has been struck by the renowned Yaśwant, whose heart is as the black bee on the lotus-foot of Lakshmikānt, to circulate through the earth. Śaka 1728" (=A.D. 1806).

8. Assam: Gaurīnātha Siṁha. AR. Wt. 88·4 grs.
   Obv., within dotted border in Bengālī script, *Śrī Śrī Gaurīnātha Siṁha nṛipasya*, "(Coin) of the king, Śrī Gaurīnātha Siṁha."
   Rev, *Śrī Śrī Hara-Gaurīpadaparasya*, "Devoted to the feet of Hara and Gaurī."

9. East India Company. Murshidābād. In the name of Shāh ʻĀlam II. AR. Rupee (machine struck).
   Obv., legend as No. 1, no date.
   Rev., as No. 1, but mint, Murshidābād, and Company's mark cinquefoil.

10. Sikh. Amritsar S. 1837. AR. Rupee.
    Obv., corrupt Persian couplet (?) *Sar tegh-i-Nānak . . . az faẓl-i fatḥ-i-Gobind Singh Saḥā* (?) *Shāhān ṣāḥib sikka zad bar sīm u zar* (?).
    Rev., *Ẓarb-i-Śrī Ambratsar julūs-i-takht ākāl sambat 1835*, "Struck at Amritsar, the accession to the eternal throne, in the Sambat year, 1835."

Note—In the Plate the obverse and reverse of No. 7 have been transposed.